College, Chapel and Culture in Edwardian Manchester

The diary of Frank C. Davidson (1883-1937)
in his first term of training
for the Primitive Methodist Ministry

COLLEGE, CHAPEL and CULTURE in EDWARDIAN MANCHESTER

The diary of Frank C. Davidson (1883-1937) in his first term of training for the Primitive Methodist Ministry

Edited by

Rachel Larkinson

Published in the UK
by the Wesley Historical Society

Website: www.wesleyhistoricalsociety.org.uk
22 Broadway Road, Evesham, WR11 1BG, England

First published, 2016

ISBN 978-0-9928762-1-0

Printed and available from Lulu.com

COLLEGE, CHAPEL and CULTURE in EDWARDIAN MANCHESTER

The diary of Frank C. Davidson (1883-1937)
in his first term of training
for the Primitive Methodist Ministry

Edited by

Rachel Larkinson

Published in the UK
by the Wesley Historical Society

Website: www.wesleyhistoricalsociety.org.uk
22 Broadway Road, Evesham, WR11 1BG, England

First published, 2016

ISBN 978-0-9928762-1-0

Printed and available from Lulu.com

To Roger, George, Andrew and Penny

With thanks for all their love and support

Frontispiece: Rev Frank Collen Davidson (Family collection)

Preface

The primary interest of this diary is in the text itself, which provides an authentic witness to events over four months in 1902, ranging from personal impressions to descriptions of the life of a ministerial student in the Methodist Church, and encompassing many references to external aspects of Manchester life.

The complete text of the diary has been carefully reproduced therefore, with only two changes, for the sake of clarity. Firstly, the heading for each day's entry has been standardised, to give the day of the week and the date. Very often in the original, only the day of the week is given for several entries on end, and it is difficult to keep track of the actual date. For ease of reference therefore, the full date is given each time.

The other change is that, for the sake of clarity, Biblical references are standardised and presented in the accepted modern form. In the diary itself, where they are given, Roman numerals are often used for chapters and the punctuation is variable.

The process of editing has involved considerable research, since many of the individuals and places mentioned are no longer familiar to people over a hundred years later. In selecting which material to provide, I have used the following principles:

1. To provide explanation of aspects that would otherwise be obscure.
2. To expand and illuminate the experience of the writer of the diary by providing background information.
3. To give biographical information for the people mentioned, which will both reflect their character and indicate their significance.
4. To provide a fuller picture of the ethos, workings and achievements of the Primitive Methodist Connexion at this time, based on what emerges from the diary.
5. To place this picture within the wider scope of nonconformity and the ecumenical scene.

During the exploration of the material that pertained to this diary, I have learned much about the religious and political factors of the early part of the twentieth century that shaped the experiences of those of us who lived through the second half of the century. I hope that the information provided here may give others some access to greater understanding too.

I have been grateful for the help of many individuals and organisations in the preparation of this book and I apologise to those I fail to mention by name, whose help has nevertheless been invaluable. The John Rylands University Library in Manchester, the Cambridge University Library, the Cambridge Divinity Faculty Library, the Cambridge City Library, Wesley House Library, Cambridge and the Cambridgeshire Local Archives have been extensively used; I have also received assistance from Emily Burgoyne at the Angus Library, Regent's Park College in Oxford and Helen Weller, Archivist, at Westminster College Library in Cambridge. Dr Jill Barber, at the Englesea Brook Museum of Primitive Methodism, has kindly facilitated access to their archives.

The Committee of the Wesley Historical Society have given their time to read the drafts and offer useful advice, and my special thanks must go to David J. Jeremy, Emeritus Professor at Manchester Metropolitan University, whose interest led me to embark on the project of editing the diary and who has kept in touch throughout with advice and encouragement. Edward Royle, Emeritus Professor at York University, has kindly read and commented upon the introduction, Dr David Ceri Jones has read through everything and made many helpful suggestions and Dr Clive Field has supplied some relevant material.

Then there are the many friends and relatives who have read parts of my work and offered observations and useful information. Rev. Dr Brian Beck expressed his interest in the diary and gave some initial help with resources, and my sister Alison and cousin Isobel have supplied some family documents and photographs to be used. Finally I must thank my husband Roger for his help with photography, his technical assistance with the computer, his patience, when I have been engaged in this time-consuming task, and his constant interest and encouragement, all of which have enabled me to bring the work to completion.

Rachel Larkinson
Cambridge
February 2016

x

Contents

List of Illustrations xii

Abbreviations xiv

Introduction 1
1. Description of the Diary 2
2. Provenance 3
3. The Purpose of the Diary 3
4. Family Background and Life of Frank Collen Davidson 4
5. The History of the Primitive Methodist Connexion 10
6. The Manchester Primitive Methodist College 11
7. The City of Manchester in 1902 23
8. The 1902 Education Bill 25
9. Characteristics of a diary 29

The Diary 39

Illustrations 114

Postscript 150

Appendices:
1. Students 1902-3: First and Second-year students 152
2. The 1902 Conference: Ministerial Education 153
3. Examination Papers of the Manchester College 156
4. Syllabus for Probationer Ministers 162
5. Extracts from Minutes of Probationers' Committee 163
6. Details of Local Preachers' Training 165
7. Extract from the Lectures of A. S. Peake 168
8. Work with Children 169

Bibliography 174

List of Illustrations

Front and back covers:
A. Manchester PM College (later named Hartley): front door
B. The Rev. Frank C. Davidson (vignette)
C. Side view of college (from Gowan Road)
Frontispiece: Rev. Frank Collen Davidson

1. Excerpt from diary
2. The Rev. James Davidson
3. Martha Ann Davidson (*née* Collen)
4. The Collen family of Soham, Cambridgeshire
5. Cecil Davidson (brother)
6. FCD with his brother Victor
7-8. A typical postcard from Cecil to FCD
9. FCD's certificate (at age 17)
10. Soham Fen (ex-PM) Methodist Chapel (no longer in use)
11. Soham Great Fen
12. Group of Primitive Methodists at Fakenham, including James Davidson
13. George and Mary Sculpher (parents-in-law)
14. Hardingham Hall Farm
15. Wedding couple, FCD and Alice Mary Sculpher
16. Hingham (ex-PM) Methodist Chapel
17. FCD as a student, with two fellow-students
18. FCD as a probationer minister, with an unknown person at Biddulph, Staffordshire
19. FCD in garden
20. FCD and Alice, with Reginald and Morley
21. Alice with Morley, Reginald and Kathleen (left to right)
22. Manse, 19 Beaconsfield Road, Basingstoke, with Kathleen
23. Alice and FCD with children Reginald, Morley, Kathleen, and Dorothy
24. Four generations: Martha Davidson, FCD, Reg, Dennis
25. Gravestone, Soham Cemetery, Cambridgeshire
26. and 27. Stow Bedon Station, Norfolk, the place from where the journey to Manchester started
28. The Manchester PM College in Alexandra Road
29. The Manchester PM College building, now a school
30. Two wings of the college, showing the rows of studies and bedrooms

31. The lecture hall
32. College photo, 1902
33. Rev. William Johnson
34. Rev. Daniel Neilson
35. Rev. Robert Hind
36. Rev. Arthur Beavan
37. Rev. John Harryman Taylor
38. Rev. Walter Graham
39. Dr Arthur S. Peake
40. Memorial inscription at the college
41. Great Western Street Methodist Chapel (ex-PM)
42. Oxford Road, with Union Chapel
43. Maclaren's pulpit – in the Union Chapel at Fallowfield
44. Brookbottom: the schoolroom, now a house
45. Brookbottom: window of the chapel where FCD preached
46. Brookbottom: countryside
47. Manchester Royal Exchange
48. Piccadilly, Manchester
49. Oxford Street PM Chapel, Blackburn
50. London Road PM Chapel, King's Lynn
51. Manchester Town Hall
52. Manchester Cathedral, 1903
53. Manchester, Whitworth Art Gallery
54. Manchester, Market Street from Cross Street, 1902
55. 1912 floods, Stowmarket
56. Stowmarket PM Chapel
57. Meeting at Stowmarket, with FCD and his father James Davidson
58. A postcard of Station Road, Petersfield, where FCD was minister 1912-15
59. Fincham, Norfolk, where FCD was minister 1915-21
60. Basingstoke PM Chapel where FCD was minister 1921-4
61. Buckenham Memorial PM Chapel, Fakenham, where FCD was minister 1928-32
62. Swaffham PM Chapel. FCD minister 1932-5
63. Manea: PM Chapel, where FCD was minister 1935-7
64. High Street, Manea, Cambridgeshire
65. Annual Assembly, Bury St. Edmunds, 1909
66. PM Synod held in 1914 at Aquila Road, Jersey

67. 1932 Middlesbrough Conference Group: FCD, Rev. F. A. Ingham, Mr E. A. Harvey, JP, Mr A. J. Deeks, Mr J. W. Able, and Mrs J. B. Hart
68. The last PM Conference Agenda, June 1932
69. Class Ticket at Methodist Union, 1932

Abbreviations

BDE: *Biographical Dictionary of Evangelicals*, ed. Timothy Larsen (Leicester: Inter-Varsity Press, 2003).

CE: Christian Endeavour (see Diary n. 72).

CUP: Cambridge University Press.

FCD: Frank Collen Davidson.

KJV: King James Version of the Bible.

JRUL: John Rylands University Library, Manchester.

OED: *Oxford English Dictionary.*

ODNB: *Oxford Dictionary of National Biography* edited by H. C. G. Matthew and Brian Harrison (Oxford: Oxford University Press, 2004).

OUP: Oxford University Press.

PM: Primitive Methodist.

PSA: Pleasant Sunday Afternoon (see Diary n. 54).

WM: Wesleyan Methodist.

INTRODUCTION

The summer of 1902 was a time of change and hope. The long Victorian era had come to an end, a new king was to be crowned, the South African war, which had absorbed 450,000 troops, was over; technological developments and the use of electricity were now transforming everyday life and, in all, the prosperity and progress of the previous century looked set to continue. To a young man leaving home for the first time, it would undoubtedly have seemed that a wealth of opportunities and new experiences lay ahead. In early August of that year, my grandfather, Frank Collen Davidson (hereafter referred to by his initials FCD) set out from the small Norfolk village of Rockland, just before his nineteenth birthday, to make the train journey to the city of Manchester, where he was to start his training to be a Methodist minister at the Primitive Manchester Theological Institute, the college that was renamed in 1906 'Hartley College' after its benefactor William Hartley.

Even the journey took him into a different world. After marvelling at the architectural magnificence of Lincoln Cathedral, he was stunned by the grandeur of the Peak District and then as the train approached Manchester, he was suddenly in a world of busy streets and city buildings. So he arrived at the college, a fine building with spacious accommodation offering wide-ranging training, from Greek and Hebrew classes to the practical experience of ministry. Ahead lay an eventful term, full of new experiences.

It has been a journey of exploration also for me to transcribe and edit his diary, because, after he left college in 1904 and serving in several circuits, he died in 1937, aged only fifty-four, some years before I was born. Until recently, I had known of him only through passing comments from my parents, so I had built up a picture of someone who was serious and committed, but not much fun and given to ill-health (although that was because their memory of him was coloured by his final illness). So it was quite a discovery to find that he was good at football and interested in art and music, with a fine bass singing voice. He seems to have worked hard, but even so took time off to attend a performance of *Messiah* the night before his last examination!

He kept the diary for his first term only, starting when he set out by train in early August from the station at Stow Bedon, a village in mid-

Norfolk, and ending when he arrived home over four months later to spend Christmas with his family. It is interesting to read his descriptions of college life, of the Principal and Tutors (who included the well-known Biblical scholar A. S. Peake) and his fellow students, of the mission he took part in and the places he visited to preach or attend worship, but also to learn how he spent his leisure time, the people he met, the art galleries and museums he visited and the performers he heard in concerts. At the same time, we pick up something of the issues that were live at the time, such as the Nonconformist opposition to the Education Bill, and incidental details such as what happened when he rode on an electric tram for the first time and the roller slipped the wire and all were plunged into darkness! He speaks of the deaths in that year of Dr Joseph Parker and Rev. Hugh Price-Hughes, two giants of Nonconformity, and recounts in detail the sermons he heard at various churches, which gives an interesting insight into religious thought at the time. All in all, there is a perhaps surprising breadth to his work, activities and interests, which speaks well of the Primitive Methodist Connexion in his day and may redress some of the pre-conceptions that people may have held about 'the Prims' in later years.

1. Description of the diary

The outward appearance of the diary is unremarkable; it is a notebook measuring 7 x 4½ inches, with an outer cover of cardboard covered by cloth and coloured a shiny black. The pages are sewn together and the lines are $3/10$ of an inch apart. There is no indication of the manufacturer of the notebook; it would seem to be an ordinary notebook purchased for the task. Apart from his name on the inside cover, there is no other heading or indication of purpose. It begins with the heading of the first day, 4 August, in ink, to which he has added 1902 in pencil. The whole diary is written in black ink, in neat legible handwriting (see illustration 1). The paper has aged and is now light brown in colour.

By the end of the first term, when the diary ends, more than half of the notebook had been used, but the rest has been left blank, perhaps indicating that he intended to take up writing it again. However, no other entries have been found.

2. Provenance

After my mother died in 1994, preparations were underway to sell the house in Fakenham, Norfolk, where she and my father had lived in retirement. Amongst the papers and other possessions stored in the eaves of the chalet-style house, my husband and I came across this diary, and took it away, along with other Methodist photographs and memorabilia. It has stayed in my possession as we moved from manse to manse, but it is only since my retirement in 2011 that I have had a chance to look at it properly and realise its interest and value.

It is not certain how it came to be in my mother's possession. She was the third of four children and, when the family moved to Manea, Cambridgeshire, in 1935, for what was to be her father's last appointment, she had recently left school and taken a secretarial course. Soon he became seriously ill and she helped him with administrative work, as well as driving him to appointments so that he could continue working as long as possible. When he died in 1937, she may well have helped to clear his study and she may have come across the diary in a drawer and decided to keep it.

The other possible explanation is that it stayed with my grandmother when she moved to Taverham, Norfolk, after her husband's death. Then in 1955 she moved again, to live with her daughter (my mother) and when she died in 1961, it was found among her possessions by my mother, who then kept it. Neither my sister nor I knew of the existence of the diary before 1994 when both our parents died, as no mention had ever been made of it.

3. The purpose of the diary

The diary was not a confessional on the pattern of earlier Nonconformist diaries, but rather, it seems, a record of events. For one who had just arrived in the city of Manchester, after growing up in rural Norfolk, there were so many new experiences, important places to visit and people to hear that it must have seemed necessary to note everything down in order to remember it all.

FCD seems to have made a particular point of noting down the text and content of sermons he heard from Methodist and other Nonconformist preachers, and so it may be that he felt this would be a help in his spiritual life and indeed his own sermon preparation in the

3

future. Perhaps he also wanted to remember the details of his life in Manchester for illustration in his own sermons.

On the whole, though, it seems he just wanted to tell someone about his life and experiences and, being away from home and on his own, writing a diary was a good substitute activity. He seems to have written it as though he was talking to a close friend or family member. For example, when describing Oxford Place Chapel, Blackburn, he compared its size to London Road Chapel in King's Lynn, which would have been known to his family and friends in Norfolk. The following term, life may have become rather busier with work and sport, and perhaps not so much new was happening to warrant recording, and so he ceased to write down day-to-day events in the diary.

4. The family background and life of Frank Collen Davidson (FCD)

On both sides of the family, roots were in rural East Anglia. The middle name 'Collen' was his mother's maiden name and a very common surname in the Soham area of Cambridgeshire where his maternal grandfather, James Collen, was a farmer with 87 acres at Great Fen Drove.[1]

His mother, Martha Ann Collen was born in Soham on 12 May 1858, the second child in a family of six. The family were strong supporters of the Primitive Methodist movement. Foundation stones at the Primitive Methodist Chapel at Soham, which was rebuilt on the site of the former chapel in 1869, were laid by family members Robert and Josiah Collen; then one of the foundation stones of Soham Fen Chapel in Great Fen Drove, which was rebuilt in 1872, was laid by John Collen, who was probably Martha's grandfather. The baptism of Martha Ann Collen, daughter of James and Emily Collen, is recorded in the Baptism Register for Soham Fen Primitive Methodist Chapel on 16 June 1858.[2] FCD is recorded as being born at Soham Fen in 1883, so it would seem that Martha went back to her family home for the birth of her first son. Her husband, James, who was himself a Primitive Methodist minister, was stationed at Diss in Norfolk at the time.

James Davidson, father of FCD, was born in 1854 at Briston, a village in north Norfolk.[3] It is thought in the family that the Davidsons came from Scotland originally, although they have been traced back in Norfolk to Joshua Davidson, born in nearby Stody in 1761. James' parents, Huson and Tamar Davidson, were both born in Norfolk and they were ordinary, honest working people, who lived in a cottage near Dalling Hall in Norfolk. Census records show that James had four brothers: William and George, who were older than him, both died young, George at the age of twelve from a gunshot wound in his hand, which became infected, and William from tuberculosis when he was eighteen. James was nine when George died and fourteen at the time of William's death, both of which family tragedies must have had their impact on him. He had two younger brothers, Charles and George (again), who was born after the older George had died and given the same name, as was a common custom. James had some education at a village school but left at the age of eleven to start work as an agricultural labourer, as did his brothers. His mother was said to have been an influence on his life, and he began attending the small Primitive Methodist chapel at Wood Dalling in the Aylsham Circuit. Inspired by the preaching, he made a commitment to Christ on Christmas evening 1868, became a member, and was preaching by the time he was seventeen years old. Successive ministers helped him with his studies and he was able to pass the examinations necessary to candidate for the ministry.

In 1876 James Davidson was accepted for training at the Sunderland Institute,[4] which was the place where Primitive Methodist ministers were trained before the Manchester college opened.[5] After training at Sunderland for a year, and four years' probation, he was recognised as an accredited itinerant preacher. He served in the following East Anglian circuits: Ipswich, Colchester, Downham Market, Watton, Rockland (twice), Diss, Wymondham, Kelsale, Aylsham, Docking (twice), King's Lynn, Wells, Swaffham,[6] St. Neots and Ely. Sometimes he would stay only a couple of years in a place, as was common in those days. He was known for his steady, conscientious work, and his genial, peaceable manner. Illness forced him to superannuate, and he retired to Soham, his wife's home, where he lived only a few weeks before he died in 1917.

James Davidson and Martha Ann Collen were married in 1882. They had probably met when he was stationed at Downham Market in 1880 and went to the little chapel at Soham Fen to preach. FCD, the oldest of four sons, was born on 9 August 1883, followed by Cecil in 1890, Arthur in 1893 and Victor in 1898. Cecil and Arthur (who died in his thirties) became schoolteachers and Victor went to work in London, though he returned to Soham in his later years. FCD was particularly close to Cecil and there survive affectionate postcards sent between them, discussing books, music and photography.

As his father was a Primitive Methodist minister, who in those days moved every one, two or three years, FCD must have had a fairly disrupted education. It is recorded that he attended school in Aylsham in Norfolk, from where he won a scholarship to King's Lynn Technical School. There he won a prize for Science and English – a leather-bound book, entitled 'A History of Our Own Times',[7] embossed on the front cover with the school motto: *Labor omnia vincit*.[8] He also gained a University of Cambridge certificate, awarded to 'Senior students who are not members of the University' in December 1900. It states that he satisfied the examiners in Arithmetic and (1) Gospel (2) English (Composition, Grammar and Geography) (3) French (4) Pure Mathematics (5) Theoretical and Practical Chemistry, Electricity and Magnetism (6) Freehand and Model Drawing (see illustration 9).

His father was stationed in King's Lynn in 1899, but then moved on to Downham Market in 1900. So the 1901 census shows him, now seventeen, lodging with a Mr and Mrs Walsh in Church Street, King's Lynn, where he was presumably continuing his studies at the Technical School. Little else is known about his childhood and youth, except that we learn from the diary that he had been on holiday to Staithes in Yorkshire, and visited London where he attended worship at the City Temple. His holidays during his childhood were usually spent on his grandfather's farm at Soham Fen, where he played with children his own age in the extended family.[9] He always seemed closer to his mother's family than to his father's relatives, who lived in the countryside north of Norwich. By the time he started his training for the ministry, his father was stationed at Rockland St. Peter in central Norfolk.

After completing his training, he went first to an appointment in Biddulph in Staffordshire[10] and then served in eight more circuits, mostly in East Anglia, but also including Petersfield and Basingstoke in Hampshire. These are listed as Stowmarket (1908), Petersfield (1912), Fincham (1915), Basingstoke (1921), Stowmarket (1924), Fakenham (1928), Swaffham (1932) and Manea (1935).[11]

In December 1909, at Hingham Primitive Methodist Chapel, he married Alice Sculpher from a Norfolk farming family who were also strong Primitive Methodists,[12] and they had four children: Reginald, Morley, Kathleen and Dorothy. Little is remembered about their family life, except that for the long summer holidays FCD would go back to his family home in Soham for some peace and rest, while his wife would take the children to her family's farm at Hardingham in mid-Norfolk, where they had a wonderful time bringing in the harvest and free from the usual constraints of being 'the minister's children'.

He lived to see Reginald and Morley married to Olive and Helen respectively, and two of his grandchildren, Dennis and Jean, were born before his premature death in November 1937. A circuit plan from Manea shows that he baptised Jean himself early in 1937. After his death, Kathleen married Thomas (Tom) Newton and Dorothy married William (Bill) Boyd, and five more grandchildren were born, Rachel and Alison (to Kathleen and Tom), Isobel (a second daughter for Morley and Helen), and Gavin and Anne (to Dorothy and Bill).

As well as serving some years as Superintendent Minister, he was active in the District. He was District Chapel Building Secretary and secretary to the Lynn and Cambridge District Synod.[13] He attended the last Conference of the Primitive Methodist Connexion at Middlesbrough in June 1932 as a representative of the Lynn and Cambridge District, and the Uniting Conference in London in September 1932.[14] He was President of Fakenham Free Church Council and his interests are listed as music and games.[15] He gave particular emphasis to the work with young people through Christian Endeavour and Sunday School. It is said of him that he was 'a capable preacher, a diligent pastor, a wise leader of men, and a most delightful friend'.[16]

At the time of his death in 1937, he was Superintendent of the Manea Circuit in Cambridgeshire. When he came to Manea in 1935, he had recently undergone an operation for cancer, and it is recorded in the Minutes of the Quarterly (Circuit) Meeting that he was unable to take up the work in the September. A letter of sympathy was sent to him at the manse. This situation continued for the rest of the Connexional year, but he was sufficiently recovered to be present at the meeting in September 1936. At this time negotiations were taking place to combine the Manea Circuit with Upwell and Outwell.

He continued in reasonable health for just over a year, but the last occasion on which he took an active part in a service was on 6 October 1937, when he rose from his sick bed to attend an important business meeting and rally. He had to leave the meeting before it was over and return to bed. He died on the afternoon of Friday 5 November.

The funeral took place at Station Road Methodist Church in Manea, with a large number of people present and five ministers taking part.

7

Among them was Rev. Ernest Fisher, his friend from college, then a minister at Whittlesey, Cambridgeshire. The hymns were 'We love the place, O God' and 'Jesu, lover of my soul.' Each circuit in which he had ministered was represented, except Petersfield and Basingstoke. He is buried in the cemetery at Soham, among the family graves. The inscription on the grave reads: 'Underneath are the everlasting arms.' When his wife died in 1961, she was buried with him and an additional inscription reads: 'Resting in thy love.'

After his death, the family received many letters of sympathy, including a particularly poignant one from Ernest Fisher, who had been a friend for most of his life. He wrote to my grandmother of him:

> I have always had a very high regard for your husband ever since I have known him. His father[17] was always a welcome visitor to my father's house[18] and for his conscientiousness and fine character we held him in honour. Frank always had his father's nobility in character although with a certain difference in personality. Frank has done some fine loyal service in our church without any pretence of doing much, and certainly without the world's plaudits and rewards. For all that I know he was appreciated among his brother ministers for his uprightness and kindness of heart … I have always retained an affection for him since I knew him in college … I have had Mr Brake[19] over this afternoon, and we are trying to make arrangements to come on Tuesday. I think we shall be able to come to the service at Manea. We feel we would like to pay our last tribute of affection to an old college chum and faithful brother in the ministry of our church.

Another letter was from Rev. John Norton[20] who was in the same year at the college and is mentioned in the diary.[21] He came originally from Norfolk, but in 1937 was minister in Frome in Somerset. He wrote:

> He was in college with me and though our paths have been far apart I always remembered him and his gracious and conscientious way – I'm afraid he worked too hard in the circuits. Following him after some years in the Petersfield Circuit and hearing of him and how he cycled those long hills, I can well imagine how it must have told on his

strength ... I enquired about him when I was in Norfolk in August and was assured that he was better so I hoped he would be able to go on for years yet. But it was not to be. May God sustain you all.

The letter from Rev. F. G. Starling,[22] another minister born in Norfolk, dated 22 November 1937, makes interesting reference to the candidating process. He wrote from Nottingham:

How well I remember the day when Frank and I left our village homes together to take the Oral Examinations in London. We met again at the District Exams in Watton, since when our ways have mostly been separated by long distances. But I have always watched with real interest his work.

A minister who was distantly related to him, Rev. Frank Collen,[23] who grew up in Soham Fen, wrote to my grandmother on 9 November 1937 from Leeds:

I am deeply sorry to learn of your sad loss ... As doubtless you know, his mother came from the same little remote spot as I did and when we were boys and youths your husband and I were very friendly when he came for his holidays. I greatly valued his friendship and I thought very highly of him and though our ways have been far apart in these last thirty years I have always retained my interest in and affection for him ...

The words in his will, written when he knew he was seriously ill, perhaps sum up his graciousness and faith:

I give and bequeath unto my dear wife, Alice Mary Davidson (2 Homeland Villas, Cley Road, Swaffham, Norfolk) all my earthly estate, absolutely. I place on record my loving appreciation of her affection and help to me and our beloved children, during married life, and pray that God's constant blessing and counsel will be given to them, each and all, until we meet again in Heaven.
(Signed) Frank Collen Davidson.

5. The history of the Primitive Methodist Connexion

The Primitive Methodist Connexion was a branch of Methodism which had developed in the early nineteenth century. Within decades of John Wesley's death, some Methodists felt that their movement, which was now a separate denomination, was becoming too like a formal church and losing the fire and enthusiasm of the open-air preaching which had brought so many converts in John Wesley's day. Men such as Hugh Bourne and William Clowes in the Staffordshire Potteries, heard of the Camp Meetings in America, great evangelical gatherings in the open air that resulted in many converts, and resolved to hold them in England. The first was at Mow Cop in May 1807. Such camp meetings were considered by the Wesleyan Methodists to breach the rules of Methodist discipline and were forbidden by the Conference of 1807. However, the leaders of this new venture felt convinced that this way of evangelism was the work of God which they could not in conscience abandon and therefore, when they were expelled from the Wesleyan Connexion, they began the new movement, which came to be called 'Primitive Methodist'. The name reflected the fact that they considered themselves to be true to the origins of Methodism, recalling John Wesley's words that he considered himself a 'Primitive Christian'. The first plans and class tickets were issued in 1811.

With evangelistic thrusts down the Trent Valley and then across to Lincolnshire, to the East Riding of Yorkshire, up to north-eastern England and down to East Anglia, Primitive Methodism expanded rapidly, so that by the time the centenary of the first camp meeting was celebrated in 1907, it could list 25 Districts, 741 Circuits, 5,126 Societies, 4,905 Preaching places, 1,153 Ministers, 16,259 Local Preachers, 210,173 Members, 4,209 Sunday Schools, 61,275 Teachers and 477,114 Scholars.[24] It had a Connexional and District organisation which mirrored the Wesleyans, although there was always a much stronger emphasis on lay leadership and giving opportunity to uneducated workers. It was said that Primitive Methodism consisted primarily of the working classes, with a sprinkling of clerks and shopkeepers, farmers and schoolmasters,[25] along with a few businessmen, and that is the experience of my family, where some were comparatively wealthy farmers, some schoolteachers, and others agricultural labourers.

By the early twentieth century, the divisions in Methodism, which meant that a large village might have three Methodist chapels in it, were seen as a hindrance to mission, and so moves towards unity were developed. This was finally brought about in 1932, when Wesleyan, Primitive and United Methodists came together to form the 'Methodist Church'. At the time of Union, the Primitive Methodist Church had 222,021 members, the Wesleyans had 517,551, and the United Methodist Church had 179,527.[26]

6. The Manchester Primitive Methodist College, later named Hartley College[27]

i) The Early Years of Primitive Methodist Ministerial Training

The Primitive Methodist Connexion did not have its own residential ministerial training until 1865 when Elmfield College was opened in York and temporarily served this purpose. Then, in 1868, what became known as the Sunderland Institute was opened, to provide one-year basic courses for ministerial students. The main source of income was the fees paid by students, which were often met by their friends or the circuits that sponsored them. The amount, £15 a year,[28] was a considerable sum in those days and the minutes[29] tell of one student, who was robbed on his journey to college, 'and his friends can ill afford the loss', being given a reduction. On the other hand another student, who had left to join the Church of England, was to be pursued for the full amount, and the more urgently since he was about to embark as a missionary to China!

However there was felt to be the need for a larger, more central training facility and Manchester, situated in an area of Primitive Methodist strength, was chosen as the location for the new college.[30] The foundation stone was laid in 1878 and the first ten students were admitted in 1881. Shortly after this, training ceased at Sunderland and the building was sold for £1,000. In the Manchester college there was accommodation for 30 students, but this soon proved inadequate for the needs of stations, and in 1895 an extension was added, duplicating the study block and providing a new dining-hall, lecture room and common room. Now 60 students would be able to be trained at the same time and the course was extended to two years, with the hope of even three years in time to come.

ii) The Manchester College

The description given in the diary of the impressive college building accords with photographs and drawings of the time.[31] A sketch of the library shows a lofty and spacious room, pleasantly furnished with chairs, tables and bookshelves. The chapel, with its stained glass windows, was not constructed until the further extension work undertaken in 1906.

Financially the Manchester College struggled in its early years. The main income was from the fees of £15 a year[32] paid by the students. The college also received some Connexional grants and tried to appeal to the Districts for funding, but with little response. It was the generosity of William Hartley,[33] after whom the college was named in 1906, which enabled the 1895 extension and the further extension in 1906 to be built.

As the number of students increased, so the teaching staff needed to be augmented. In 1892, A. S. Peake[34] joined the staff and developed courses in Biblical Studies to a standard that would come to be recognised by the University of Manchester.[35]

It was not just the high standard of the courses that was so impressive during Arthur Peake's time, but also the rigorous attention to biblical criticism and the importance of the study of the ancient languages. From the beginning, a lot had been asked of students who might have had little formal education before arriving at college. The syllabus for 1883 gives an idea of the scope of the education then.[36] Theology was studied from Angus' *Handbook to the Bible*, and an examination task on this was: 'State what is meant by systematic and inferential study of the scripture.' In addition, students were examined on Milner's *English History*,[37] Wayland's *Moral Science*,[38] Cornwell's *Geography*,[39] Kidder's *Homiletics*, Milner's *Church History*, Whateley's *Rhetoric*, Colenso's *Arithmetic*, Watson's *Theology*, Whateley's *Logic*, Morrell's *English Grammar*, and Primitive Methodist history. It was a broad syllabus the aim of which was to produce well-educated young men who could preach with knowledge and conviction and hold their own in discussion in the world. However, in Peake's view this curriculum was 'antiquated and reactionary'.[40]

What was missing was a detailed study of the Biblical text and Peake worked to rectify that. By 1897 the list of subjects to be examined included Greek, Hebrew, German, Old Testament exegesis,

12

New Testament exegesis, Introduction to Old and New Testaments, and for any third years, textual criticism, Johannine theology and the history of religion. Not many of the students took examinations in Hebrew, but the highest mark achievable by those taking the English alternative was 80%. With this syllabus, the students were given a thorough and balanced grounding in the Bible and the results were far-reaching, in that the extremes of fundamentalism were avoided in Primitive Methodism.

By 1902, the needs of the stations (or appointments) in the country meant that Conference asked the college to take an extra ten students; this meant an intake of forty students and there were already 30 going into the second year. So, with a grant from the connexion and further generous financial help from William Hartley, an extra tutor was employed. The minutes of the committee of 29 May 1902 give the following staffing arrangements, which would cover the period of FCD's diary:

> Principal: G. Parkin
> Vice-Principal: W. Johnson
> Lector: A. S. Peake
> Additional Lector: D. Neilson

A committee met on 25 June to consider the work of the new tutor and allocated to him: New Testament Greek, Psychology, Logic, Essays (English), and, after Christmas, New Testament exegesis, and perhaps Classical Greek. An English Literature class was also added after Christmas. Perhaps it was because of uncertainties about Rev. D. Neilson's health that Rev. A. L. Humphries in fact took up the appointment of Additional Tutor, and in the diary is introduced as the new tutor.

iii) The College Staff

It might have been thought that the Primitive Methodist Connexion would have had difficulty in staffing such a college with lecturers of suitable academic qualifications, especially in view of the fact that it was only in 1871 that the abolition of religious tests made it possible for non-Anglicans to study Divinity at Oxford, Cambridge and some other universities. However, there was in fact no lack of highly qualified staff to teach the students. It is clear from the biographies of the staff in 1902 given below that some older ministers had, in home or circuit life, been afforded the opportunity to study in Scotland or

Ireland, where there was no bar to Nonconformists, and the younger ones, through scholarships and exceptional ability, had been able to study at Oxford or Cambridge and undertake academic work.

Principal: Rev. George Parkin MA, BD (1846-1933)[41]

George Parkin was born at Eston, near Middlesbrough. He candidated and was accepted for the Primitive Methodist Ministry, being one of the first group of students to be trained at the Sunderland Theological Institute. He began his ministry in Glasgow in 1869 and spent his first ten years in Scottish missions. During this time he gained MA and BD degrees from Glasgow University, one of the first PM ministers to graduate. He then had successful ministries in Glasgow, Wishaw, Leeds, Chesterfield and Northampton, before, in 1898, becoming principal of the Theological Institute in Manchester, later to be named Hartley College. He was also tutor in Hebrew. In 1903 he moved to a circuit appointment in Oldham and during his time there, in 1906, he was President of Conference. In 1908 he gave the Hartley lecture on 'The New Testament Portrait of Jesus'. Then in 1914 he retired to Manchester, for a time helping in the Manchester VI Circuit at Withington, where he lived. He died in January 1933, one of the oldest and most honoured ministers of the Primitive Methodist Connexion.

Vice-Principal: Rev. William Johnson (1844-1919)[42]

William Johnson was born on 11 February 1844 in Halifax, though his parents soon moved to Shipley, where he spent his childhood. His father, George, who worked as a wool comber in the local factory,[43] was a Local Preacher, and his mother a strong influence on his life. After his conversion at the age of seventeen, he became a Local Preacher, and in 1864 he was called into the ministry by the Maryport Circuit.

In 1903 he became Principal of the Manchester College and stayed in that position until 1908, when he went back into circuit ministry in Hull, before retiring to Ripon in 1909. Apart from his time at the college, he served in the following circuits: Maryport, Berwick, Staithes, Alston, Gateshead, Whitehaven, Hartlepool, South Shields, Gateshead (again), Shildon, Hartlepool (again) and Hull VI.[44] Far from finding the routine of a Primitive Methodist minister's life tiresome, in all these stations he gave himself fully to the work, visiting people with a courtesy and kindness that was affectionately remembered.

14

His term as Principal of the Hartley College was memorable by reason of the extensions that were carried through. The College premises were doubled in size and the number of students went up to 90. For two years workmen were never off the premises, yet through all that time the work of the college continued, and the tasks of the Principal increased. The members of the College Committee were fully aware of the great service Mr Johnson rendered at this point in the history of the College.

William Johnson had a great reputation as a preacher. People remembered his sermons, not just for the literary grace and rare homiletical skill, but most of all for the consuming passion which seemed to grip him, and which gave him power over his congregations. His faith in God and in Jesus Christ as the Divine Redeemer was his supreme creed.

After retirement to Harrogate, during the last few months of his life he suffered painful illness but his deep confidence in the love of God, his sure and certain hope of the resurrection through Christ, and his joy in the anticipation of meeting old comrades sustained him. At the funeral service, his former colleague, Prof. A. L. Humphries, offered prayer.

Lector: Arthur Samuel Peake MA (1865-1929)[45]

Arthur Samuel Peake was said to be the greatest biblical scholar of his generation.[46] His presence at the College from 1892 for over thirty years had a profound effect on the quality of the academic training given at the college and the biblical understanding with which students were equipped to go out to serve their circuits.

He was born in 1865 at Leek in Staffordshire, the son and nephew of Primitive Methodist ministers. His father, Samuel Peake (1830-1914),[47] was an evangelical preacher of the old school, able to stir a congregation to penitence and joy, a devout and faithful minister and a strict father. His mother Rosabella, from an Anglican farming family in Herefordshire, was converted under the preaching of the Primitive Methodists. It was said that from her Arthur inherited both his brilliance and his lovable nature.[48] He was very close to her in his early years, but in 1875, when he was nearly ten, she was taken ill and died. He always remembered her with great affection and wished she could have lived to see his later achievements.

Arthur was the third of six children, although his older sister, Alice, had died when she was just three, a cause of great sadness to the family.

15

His older brother, George, was a strong character, hard-working, conscientious, generous and considerate, and much admired by Arthur. He was also very fond of his younger sister Emily, who to some extent took over the role of mother in caring for the other children. The family were financially poor, and subject to the frequent moves of a Primitive Methodist minister, but Arthur flourished at school and won a Closed Scholarship from King Henry VIII's Grammar School in Coventry to St. John's College, Oxford, to read Classics.[49]

After an inauspicious start, gaining only third class in Classics Honours Moderations, he switched to Theology, in which he excelled, being awarded the Casberd Scholarship in 1887 and gaining a first class honours degree. In 1890 he secured a fellowship at Merton College, the first Nonconformist layman to be elected to a theological fellowship at Oxford. From 1890 he also taught at the Congregational Mansfield College, which had opened in Oxford with A. M. Fairbairn as Principal.

Arthur had been brought up in the evangelical Primitive Methodist religious environment, but during his years at Oxford he had been much influenced by those who taught him and from whom he learnt the value of a historical-critical approach to Biblical Studies.[50] He also owed a great debt to A. M. Fairbairn for his philosophical thinking as well as his encouragement and friendship.

His time at Oxford had opened up to him the breadth of modern scholarship in relation to the study of the Bible, and given the opportunity to make many good friends for life.[51] During that time he also joined the Oxford Socialists and was much exercised by the poverty and hardship that he heard of in London[52] and witnessed in Oxford during the harsh winter of 1890-1. He was also a staunch supporter of the Liberal Party and Gladstone's policy of Irish Home Rule.

During his years at Oxford he met his wife, Harriet Mary Sillman. They were married in June 1892 and had three sons, one of whom became a Methodist minister.[53] She was an Anglican, and, in recognition of this, their daily devotions were always from the Church of England Prayer Book, but she supported him fully in all his work and attended Primitive Methodist worship. Arthur had at one time contemplated entering the Anglican priesthood, on the grounds that only from within could one counteract ritualism, and that the Primitive Methodist ministry, with its arduous working pattern and frequent moves, would be damaging to his somewhat fragile health and also

16

prevent him from establishing himself in any field, but in the event he took neither course as different opportunities opened up for him. In May 1891 he was approached by William Hartley[54] to consider moving to Manchester to take up a position as a tutor at the Manchester Primitive Methodist Theological College. Hartley was offering to fund the appointment for five years. Arthur had long been concerned about the quality of training the Connexion's ministers received, but to accept such an appointment and leave Oxford would be quite a sacrifice for him. During that summer he spent two months in Heidelberg considering the matter, during which time he wrote to his father explaining how he felt it to be his duty to offer his services to the Connexion in this way. In 1892 he began the work in Manchester which was to occupy the rest of his life.

One of his first tasks on arrival at the Manchester College was to build up the library, which he deemed to be woefully inadequate. He appealed across the Connexion for books and laid the foundations of what was to be an outstanding library. His influence on the curriculum and the approach to biblical studies over the years that followed was immense. There may have been a few critics, who feared any departure from literal fundamentalism, but on the whole he held the confidence of the Primitive Methodists for 37 years.

In 1895 he took on tutoring at the Lancashire Independent College in addition to his current duties, and then in 1904 he accepted a lectureship at the United Methodist Free Church's Victoria Park College in Manchester. However he had in time to give both these up in view of the increasing work he was asked to undertake at the University of Manchester. In 1899 he had been appointed one of the original members of the Council of Governors of the John Rylands Library, and then in 1904 he played a key role in the establishment at the university of the Theology Faculty, of which he was the first Dean, and became the first holder of the John Rylands Chair of Biblical Criticism and Exegesis (1904-29).[55]

In addition to lecturing, he was the author of many publications, beginning in 1902 with his commentary on *Hebrews*.[56] However he is best remembered for *Peake's Commentary*, which was published in 1919, in which he says he sought to 'put before the reader in a simple form ... the generally accepted results of Biblical Criticism, Interpretation, History and Theology'. This work, although it has been republished in revised form, is still a valuable tool nearly a hundred

17

years later for those seeking a knowledge and understanding of the Scriptures. He wrote one eighth of the material himself and is said to have worked through the articles of the other 61 contributors ten times before publication. The habit of diligent and methodical study impressed upon him in his childhood, coupled with his own desire to see a task perfectly completed, served him well in these years, although the level of work he maintained may well already have been taking a toll on his health. His son commented that Christmas Day was the only day of the year that he treated as a complete holiday.[57]

Although generally welcomed, the commentary was not without its critics. Graham Scroggie, a well-known Baptist evangelical preacher described it as 'sodden with infidelity'. Peake also had to face criticism of the courses and training at Hartley from a minority of traditional evangelicals. However his personal piety, his scholarship and honesty in seeking the truth, along with his gracious nature, meant that he held the confidence of his denomination, enabling PM ministers to accept critical biblical scholarship without losing their faith,[58] and the same was true of many other church leaders. In the words of the Wesleyan, George Jackson, echoed by the New Testament scholar, C. H. Dodd, he 'saved the English Church from a fundamentalist controversy'.[59]

In 1902 he became ill and underwent an operation the outcome of which was not certain for a while, but fortunately he recovered and was able to return to work after a period of convalescence. In the minutes of the College Quarterly Committee[60] for 27 November 1902, sympathy was expressed towards him because of his illness, which might necessitate an operation. In December the committee recorded its pleasure that he was steadily improving, and in February 1903 he was congratulated on his restoration to health. His absence over some of the time of the diary may explain why there are fewer references to him than one might expect.[61]

When he died in 1929 at the age of 63, following a second operation for hyatid cysts on the liver, tributes to him flowed in from all quarters, including a letter from the Archbishop of Canterbury. Teaching had been his life, based on the conviction he had held since his Oxford days that the new approach to an understanding of Scripture should be disseminated to a wider constituency, and that this was to be done by those who were best able to spread it.[62] He had served his church loyally and faithfully at no little cost to himself. In all, he had touched so many lives with his brilliance, his integrity and his kind and

18

generous nature, but what shone through most and underpinned everything was his personal faith in Christ.

Rev. Albert Lewis Humphries MA (1865-1950)[63]
Tutor in New Testament Greek, Exegesis and Systematic Theology

Albert Lewis Humphries was born in Bristol in 1865. By means of scholarships, he was educated at Liverpool College and St. John's College, Cambridge, where he obtained his BA and MA degrees; he entered the ministry in 1887. He married first Lavinia Antliff, daughter of Rev. Samuel Antliff, who was President of the Primitive Methodist Conference in 1873. Then, after her death, his second marriage was to May Bowen of Wilmslow. He had two sons and a daughter. He served in the following circuits, before becoming a tutor at the College in 1902: Derby I, Birmingham I, Matlock, Chesterfield I.

At the College, where he taught for 33 years, influencing generations of students with his own high standards of scholarship and industry, his subjects were Greek, Psychology, New Testament Exegesis and Theology. During the First World War he also served in the Manchester Ardwick circuit. He was Secretary of the Local Preachers' Training Committee from 1910-24 and President of Conference in 1926. At Union, he became chairman of the Manchester Second District. His publications included *St. John and other New Testament Writers: The Holy Spirit in Faith and Experience*, and *Hartley College* as well as numerous articles and reviews in magazines. He retired in 1935, though he continued to serve his chapel, circuit, district and college for some years, and died on 28 March 1950 after a long life of work faithfully done.[64]

Rev. Daniel Neilson (1850-1904), Additional Lector[65]

Daniel Neilson was born at Lanark on 30 January 1850. His obituary does not give his father's occupation, though it might be assumed that he worked in the drapery business where the young Neilson found his first employment. His mother was said to be an exceptional person and it may well be that he inherited from her those elements of character which distinguished his life. The habit of study was formed early and he walked a considerable distance to the early morning classes at Glasgow University, returning to business at the proper hour. A commercial man, who observed his application and personality, placed £300 to his credit at the bank, with which he commenced business on his own account. He was successful as a draper and sacrificed considerable business prospects to enter the ministry.

When about eleven years of age, Neilson had accepted Christ as his personal Saviour in the PM Mission Room, Turner Street, Glasgow. He was an accredited Local Preacher at seventeen years of age. Then in 1872, he was sent by the Missionary Committee to Wolverhampton. His next appointment was to Tollcross, Glasgow. He married Miriam (*née* Hardy), who consistently and faithfully shared with her husband the 'duties, joys, sorrows and triumphs of ministerial life.' His next circuits were Belfast, Dublin, Belfast again, Clitheroe, Blackburn and Walkden. When he was in Dublin he eagerly utilised the opportunities the university offered, taking his BA, MA and BD degrees.

After some difficulties, he tendered his resignation from the Primitive Methodist ministry, joined the English Presbyterian Church, became a recognised minister, was engaged for a short time in mission work and was then offered a pastorate, but in 1891 was persuaded to obtain re-entry to the Primitive Methodist Connexion. For more than thirteen years he then served in the Manchester II and Manchester VI circuits.

For several years Daniel Neilson was a valuable member of the Moss Side School Board. At the time of his death he was a member of the Education Committee and General Secretary to the Probationers' Examining Committee. For nine years he acted as Assistant Classical Tutor at the PM College in Manchester, where his work was much appreciated by the students.

The Rev. W. G. Softley[66] wrote: 'I shall treasure his memory for the tremendous influence he had upon me while under his tuition in the College, and for kindly opportunity of knowing one so full of generous instincts and noble purposes, and so successful in inspiring others with his genial enthusiasm.' This is one of many testimonies to his work and worth as a tutor.

It was said of him that as a student he was methodical, painstaking and persistent, and as a preacher he presented the truth in fresh and living form. Although his many and varied commitments occupied his attention, he gave time to pastoral work. As a friend, he was said to be genial, constant, candid and reliable.

Daniel Neilson had been in failing health for some time, but there was no warning that the end of his life was so near. However, 1 October 1904, when, on a visit to his relatives at Crewe, he peacefully passed away in his sleep at the early age of 54.

20

iv) Finance and practical matters

Monthly expenditure can be seen in the Accounts of the College.[67] In August 1902, the following payments were made:

Baker: £7 1s 5d.
Fruit and Vegetables: £7 5s 0d.
Butcher: £25 11s 6d.
Hartley Preserves: £4 19s 6d.
Greens: £12 7s 9d.
Coal: £10 1s 10d.
Cheese: £1 7s 0d.
Corn for fowls: £1 2s 6d.
Tinned meat etc.: £11 5s 0d.
Chemist: £1 0s 10d.
Milk: £2 13s 4d.
Gas: £18 17s 1d.
Butter: £12 3s 6d.
Water: £7 0s 8d.

The college was centrally heated by Saunders & Taylor's Low Pressure Water Apparatus.[68]

There were, of course, the salaries and payments to staff also to be found. In addition to the academic staff, the college employed a cook, a kitchen maid, two college maids, two laundry maids, a housemaid, a gardener and a boy.

At the time of the diary, the welfare of the students, including their care when sick, was undertaken by the Vice-Principal's wife. However, she died during 1903. This evidently led to practical difficulties, since she had been carrying out various tasks voluntarily and, as a result, arrangements had to be put in place to appoint a matron who, among other duties, would care for students when they were sick.

Illness could be quite a problem in such an institution: in 1895 the December examinations had to be abandoned because so many people were sick with influenza. On other occasions special consideration had to be given to one or two students who were too ill to take all, or part of, the examinations. Sometimes it was a serious condition such as scarlet fever, which meant a student had to go home to recuperate; at other times it was insomnia and collapse under the strain of the work. Students had to attain 60% overall in the examinations and could feel

21

their whole future was at stake if they failed to do so. In such cases there would be an appeal to Conference if there were extenuating circumstances. Study and examinations continued after the student left college for a further two or three years of Probation, and at one point the syllabus was reduced for those who had left college because it was found that, with all this work, 'students were unable to give their full attention to the work of practical ministry'.[69]

v) College ethos and subsequent history

It might seem from the foregoing account that study took up a disproportionate amount of the students' time, but that does not seem to be so from FCD's diary. There appears to have been a good balance of lectures in the morning, sport or leisure in the afternoon and communal activities in the evening. FCD benefitted greatly from the opportunities to visit art galleries and attend concerts with world-class performers. He also took the opportunity to visit different Nonconformist chapels and hear the leading preachers of the day. It is notable how readily the Nonconformist churches interacted, with no mention of theological difference or rivalry, whereas he only went to hear preach one Anglican clergyman in the diary, who was against ritualism. This was a time when inter-church relationships were seen differently and Nonconformists had a confidence born of congregations and Sunday-schools that regularly numbered hundreds of members.

The motto of the college was *Ubi spiritus, ibi libertas*[70] ('Where the spirit is, there is freedom'). Life at the college seemed to enable students to experience this in preparation for the years ahead of them in circuit, when the quality of their training would be tested.

After Methodist Union in 1932, Hartley College united with Victoria Park College,[71] to form Hartley Victoria College, using the same building on Alexandra Road South. The WM College, Didsbury, continued for a while, working more closely with Hartley Victoria, but after the war the property was sold and a new college, called Didsbury at the time, opened in Bristol in 1951. Then in 1972, the decision was taken at Conference to close Hartley Victoria and sell the building, which is now a school, but the work of ministerial training continued in Manchester in conjunction with the Baptists, and later the URC as well, in the Northern Baptist College. Now called the Manchester Christian Institute, ecumenical training has continued in the premises at Luther

King House in Brighton Grove, Manchester. However, the decision of the 2012 Methodist Conference to concentrate ministerial training at two hubs in Birmingham and at Cliff College in Derbyshire, has finally brought to a close an era of fine work in Methodist theological education in Manchester.

7. The city of Manchester in 1902

Manchester in 1902 was a city of contrasts. The centre was characterised by prosperous buildings with notable architecture, reflecting the wealth that entered the city through trade and industry, but at the same time the skyline was dominated by the smoking chimneys of the many factories. These polluted the atmosphere and rendered all the buildings black.[72] The city centre boasted some fine shops, but not far away poor workers lived in abject poverty and appalling housing conditions.

The history of the city in the preceding century reflected the development of industry, especially the textile industry, because of which it earned its nickname 'Cottonopolis'. The growth was exponential; from 2,977,000 lbs. of raw cotton imported in 1751, the import rose to 99,306,000 lbs. in 1815, 488 million lbs. by 1841 and a peak of 2,648 million lbs. in 1915.[73] The subsequent decline and collapse of the cotton industry was almost as dramatic in the years after the Second World War, due to relatively high manufacturing costs and the continued rise of foreign competitors.

Population growth kept pace with the industrial history. From a city of 20,000 in the 1780s, Manchester with Salford grew to a population of almost half a million by the middle of the nineteenth century. By 1931, with the addition of suburbs like Heaton Park and Wythenshawe, the population was over a million. In recent years, the population of the inner city areas of Manchester and Salford has declined, but the population of Greater Manchester has remained at about 2.5 millions.[74]

Manchester, like other British cities in the nineteenth century, expressed its growing prosperity in imposing civic buildings. 'One can scarcely walk about Manchester without coming across frequent examples of the *grand* in architecture.'[75] The Victorian architects imitated past ages, so there were Gothic railway stations, Grecian Baptist chapels and Elizabethan tramway depots. In 1802 Thomas Harrison designed the Portico Library in Mosley Street in the classical style, imitating the Temple of Athena Polias in Ionia. The architect

23

Sir Charles Barry (who became famous for his design for the Westminster Houses of Parliament), in 1824 designed the Manchester Institute, later the City Art Gallery, in similar classical style.

The Italian Renaissance inspired buildings such as the Athenaeum, whose style provided a pattern for the great warehouses that were giving the city a new look. 'Structures fit for kings,' wrote Bradshaw in his first guide to Manchester. The internal structure was a cast iron framework, with as many large windows as possible. The warehouses showcased manufactured goods to Manchester's globally-active merchants and overseas customers and therefore needed a much more imposing architectural character than the 'dark satanic mills' where the grim business of manufacturing was done. First was 15 Mosley Street, built by Edward Walters in 1839 with a red-brick facade. Perhaps the most prominent, by Edward Walters, was 9 Portland Street, built in 1851 for James Brown & Son. The windows were richly carved. One of those still standing is the S. & J. Watts warehouse in Portland Street,[76] now the Britannia Hotel, designed by Travis & Mangnall and built at a cost of £100,000. Each floor is in a different architectural style, Egyptian, Italian Renaissance, Elizabethan and French Renaissance, topped by four roof projections with rose windows.

Edward Walters' supreme work was the Free Trade Hall, built in Peter Street in 1853 on the site of the Peterloo Massacre of 1819. It is a fine, two-storey building in the Italian renaissance style, modelled on the Gran Guardia of Verona, which Walters had visited in 1837, though the parapet and frieze are much grander than in Verona.

The new Town Hall,[77] opened in 1877 at a cost of £1,000,000 was designed by Alfred Waterhouse, who had previously designed the Assize Courts in 1859 in Venetian Gothic. He had come fourth in the competition, but his design was chosen as the least costly. It is a typically proud Victorian building in the Gothic style, with a prominent clock-tower. The main hall was decorated with a series of historical murals by Ford Madox Brown.[78] The whole building represented the wealth, industry and power that characterised Manchester at that time.

During the nineteenth century higher education was established in Manchester as a result of a large bequest from a wealthy cotton merchant, John Owens. When he died in 1846, he left £96,942 in his will, for the establishment of a college which would admit students without any test as to religious affiliation or any distinction based on rank or position in society.[79] Owens College, as it was called, began life in Quay Street in 1851, then moved to new buildings in Oxford Road, Chorlton-on-Medlock, in 1873. Some years were to pass before university status was achieved. In 1884, the government created the Victoria University, uniting Owen's College with Yorkshire College, Leeds and University College, Liverpool, and then in 1903, Manchester became a university in its own right.

The Primitive Methodist College, situated to the south of the city, near to the Alexandra Park, in 1902 was surrounded by fields, but today the buildings are to be found in a vast area of suburban housing. Art galleries, museums and shops were within walking distance, as were various Nonconformist churches serving different communities.

8. The 1902 Education Bill[80]

In the diary there are several references to the huge demonstrations and rallies that were taking place in 1902 to protest about Balfour's Education Bill. Nonconformists saw this bill as giving advantage to the Church of England, by enabling it to spread its influence further in schools and to gain financially, as rate-payers' money would be channelled into Church schools. For Nonconformists, the key issue was religious equality and it seemed to their leaders that this was the moment to seize to put right past injustices and set in place a sound policy for the future. Although the denominational question was only one aspect of a wide-ranging bill, feelings ran deep on this issue and formidable opposition to the whole bill developed. As C. H. Kelly, past President of the Wesleyan Connexion put it, 'They had no doubt they were on the side of God, of truth, and of the children.'[81]

The background to these protests was educational provision in the preceding decades. The development of state education in the late nineteenth century began with W. E. Forster's Education Act of 1870, which had provided for the establishment of the first schools under public control, the Board Schools. These were set up largely in the new urban and working-class areas where there was little voluntary provision and were popular with Nonconformists, whose ministers were often elected to the local Board. Through this a Nonconformist chapel gained wider influence in the community, and could be seen as the 'people's church'.[82]

However, over four-fifths of elementary schools had been set up by the Anglicans, and these continued to be Anglican-controlled after the 1870 Act, giving them a monopoly in many rural areas where no Board Schools were needed. Nonconformists, apart from the Wesleyans, had few schools before 1870, so it was in their interest to remove taxpayer funding from Anglican schools.

The issue went beyond education to the question of religious equality. Many held the basic principle that ecclesiastical privilege should not exist anywhere and certainly not in schools. There was the feeling that state aid to the Church of England would help it to indoctrinate children with its denominational teaching. The 1870 Bill to make education available to all had been welcomed but there was dismay amongst Nonconformists at the advantages accorded to the Anglicans.

Their cause was taken up by the National Education League, and a Central Nonconformist Committee was set up in Birmingham to organise protests against the bill. Every Nonconformist minister was asked to sign a petition to the House of Commons as a protest to Gladstone and a large proportion did so. As a concession, an amendment was added to the bill permitting School Boards to exclude any 'catechism or religious formulary' from the new schools.

Towards the end of the century there was a 'revival' in the Church of England, with a High Church emphasis that looked back to the Oxford Movement of the 1830s. It was what the Nonconformists called 'ritualism'. Priests turned east at the Eucharist, and vestments and incense became common. Some hoped for reunion with the Roman Catholic Church. At the same time religious education took a higher profile and denominational ('voluntary') schools were seen as key to this. These, in fact, were very much in need of financial support. Then a controversy in London over the teaching given in state schools on the matter of the Trinity re-ignited concerns over the Anglican influence in state schools. The Nonconformists wanted teaching to be Bible-based and together with evangelical Anglicans set up a joint Bible Education Council in 1894.

A bill passed in 1897 gave more state aid to voluntary schools, which were struggling financially, and exempted them from paying rates. However this was not enough for the Anglicans who were campaigning for all voluntary (i.e. Church) schools to receive rate aid and not have public representation on their managing bodies.[83]

Meanwhile, Nonconformist agitation was increasing, and for the first time the Free Church Councils played a significant part in the politics of the day, fighting government proposals.

In rural locations, there were still 8,000 places where the only elementary school was a Church of England school in the 1890s. Nonconformist parents had no choice but to send their children to schools where denominational teaching was given. They could withdraw their children from religious instruction, though most did not, but the whole atmosphere at school was directed towards attendance at the Anglican church. City Nonconformists sympathised with the plight of those in the countryside.

In 1902, Balfour's Act decreed that Local Authorities should assume responsibility for all state-funded elementary and secondary education. This act was a wide-ranging attempt to rationalise the elementary school system. Instead of school boards, the local authorities, working through education committees, were to run the schools. An important aspect was the provision for education beyond the Elementary (Standard VI) level. School Boards had been intended for elementary education only, though some had already set up schools teaching beyond this, and alternative government funding had been available since 1890 for technical education. Now Local Education Committees, nominated by elected borough and county councils, were to be responsible for both elementary and secondary education.[84] However this key aspect was largely forgotten by the Nonconformists in the furore created by the Education Bill over church schools.

In the 1902 Bill, denominational schools were included in the system and given rate aid, but had to have one third of their managers from the general public. This was not the complete public control that the Nonconformists wanted and there was a genuine sense of grievance that denominational teaching was to be paid for out of the rates. Not only would they be forced to pay out for the support of teaching they did not believe in, but they would be made to hand over their children to receive this teaching. 'Rome on the rates' was the emotive phrase coined by John Clifford, one of the most prominent leaders of the Dissenting protestors.[85] 'We should have to pay for the destruction of Nonconformity',[86] wrote Robertson Nicoll.

What followed was a crusade of unprecedented proportions. At the National Free Church Council meeting in London to co-ordinate the united protest, its president, Rev. W. J. Townsend of the Methodist

New Connexion denounced the new 'church rate' and demanded its withdrawal 'in the name of national righteousness'. In Leeds on 9 September 1902, 70,000 people attended a huge demonstration with speeches by sixteen MPs and others. This was typical of thousands of rallies held up and down the country, such as the one in Manchester described in this diary.

A passive resistance movement was begun whereby people withheld the proportion of their rates that went to education. Some denominations, however, held back from giving people any specific direction to take action of this kind. The Wesleyans expressed the strongest reservations, some of whom were grateful to the bill for coming to the aid of their schools. John Scott Lidgett, a leading Wesleyan educationalist, said they would not give any support to civil disobedience. Free Church Councils were divided on the issue. Eventually, a separate National Passive Resistance Committee was set up and rate refusals began in 1903. Many people were prosecuted and some even went to prison.

Support for the campaign against the Education Bill came from three places in particular, the West Riding of Yorkshire, Wales, and among the Primitive Methodists, who were the most rural of the denominations and most liable to discrimination in villages with just one school. Their Connexional Education Committee gave official endorsement to passive resistance, and the first person to be summoned for rate refusal was a Primitive Methodist farmer in Derbyshire; more Primitive Methodists went to prison than from any other denomination.[87]

Over subsequent years, after attempts to reverse the Bill had failed, Nonconformists were more ready to compromise and there were more pressing issues to hand on which Christians needed to show an united front. So in the end, the 1902 Act remained substantially in force until the Butler Education Act of 1944, and the opportunity for finding a solution to the Anglicans' widespread monopoly of rural education was lost. The Nonconformists had succeeded in drawing attention to the issues with their massive demonstrations, rallies and passive resistance, but it proved more difficult to achieve their objectives through the political process. Even in today's more ecumenically-friendly times, the legacy of this outcome is still sometimes to be seen in rural areas, more than a century later. Meanwhile, the benefits of the Bill should not be forgotten, for it laid the foundations for the rapid expansion of secondary education in the early years of the twentieth century.

9. Characteristics of a diary

A diary has a particular historical importance because it is written without the knowledge of subsequent developments, awareness of which would be likely to colour the narrative of a later, retrospective writer. So in this diary we can read of packed chapels, vibrant preachers, choirs and galleries full of young people, without there being a tinge of sadness for the empty pews and redundant buildings of the later twentieth century. As we read of the activities of this group of young students, there can be no hint of ministries cut short by sickness or stress, of ministers still preaching faithfully at the age of 80, and of which of them will become Chairman of a District or indeed President of Conference. The wonder at new technology, such as the electric car, is not dimmed by knowledge of more amazing recent achievements. Thus the diary, as well as the recording of people and events of the day, gives an insight into the mind of the writer at that moment in time, and indeed into the faith and hope of a generation.

NOTES TO THE INTRODUCTION

[1] 1881 census.

[2] Information supplied by George Ginn of Soham, who made a copy of the register before sending it to the Cambridgeshire County Archives.

[3] The main sources for James Davidson's life are the Connexional obituary in the *Minutes of the Primitive Methodist Conference 1918*, held at Wesley House, Cambridge (though his place of birth is erroneously given as Bristol instead of Briston) and an article by C. Shreeve in the *Aldersgate Magazine 1913*, p. 87, held at Englesea Brook Museum. Additional information about the family has been supplied by Beryl Rout, a descendant of James' brother, Charles.

[4] The Minutes of the Sunderland Institute Committee, now at the John Rylands Library in Manchester, for 25 May 1876, record his name and 21 others, as students to be admitted. There is an additional note stating that 'the other applicants to be informed there is not room for them'. The syllabus for Probationer ministers for this time (see Appendix 4) envisages that some will do all their studies at home, so clearly the need for the new college at Manchester, which opened its doors to its first students in 1881, was urgent.

[5] See p. 11. The first Primitive Methodist ministerial training took place from 1865 at Elmfield College, York, but this was superseded in 1868 by the Sunderland Institute. Geoffrey Milburn, *Primitive Methodism* (Peterborough: Epworth Press, 2002), pp. 39-42.

[6] The 1911 census shows him living in Swaffham, with his wife and two younger children still at home; Arthur is 18 and a pupil teacher and Victor, who is 13, is at school.

[7] Justin McCarthy, MP, *A History of Our Own Times, Fifth Volume, from 1880 to the Diamond Jubilee* (London: Chatto & Windus, 1899).

[8] 'Work conquers all', which seems a suitably improving adaptation for Victorian times of the quotation from Chaucer (1.158) *Amor vincit omnia.* This derives from Virgil, *Eclogues* 10.69, *Omnia vincit Amor. The Oxford Dictionary of Quotations* (London: Book Club Associates/OUP, 1981).

[9] See p. 9 for reference to this in the letter from a distant cousin Rev. Frank Collen, which the family received after the death of FCD.

[10] This is according to *Who's Who in Methodism 1933,* although W. Leary lists Bradley Green, near Redditch, as his first circuit, which accords with the Primitive Methodist Minutes of 1904 (held at Wesley House Library, Cambridge). *Who's Who in Methodism* is perhaps to be preferred, as FCD

was still alive at the time to supply information himself; the stations in 1904 could have been subject to last-minute change after the printing of the PM Minutes, and Leary may have derived his information from them. *Who's Who in Methodism 1933* (London: The Methodist Times and Leader, Methodist Publications Ltd., 1933); W. Leary, *Primitive Methodist Ministers and their Circuits* (Loughborough: Teamprint, 1990).

[11] Leary, *Primitive Methodist Ministers*.

[12] On her father's side, her grandfather's brother, Rev. John Sculpher (1817-1889) was an early Primitive Methodist minister who served in fifteen circuits in East Anglia. Her father, George Dennis Sculpher farmed at Hardingham Hall Farm, near Hingham, Norfolk. George was born in Cambridge, where his parents, James and Charlotte, lived briefly and attended Castle Street Primitive Methodist Church. The account in the local newspaper of the funeral of her mother, Mary Sculpher (née Morley) who died in 1925, states that both George and Mary were Local Preachers and that Mary had been a Primitive Methodist all her life and a member of Hingham Chapel for over twenty-five years, ever since the family moved to Hardingham from Rougham, Norfolk, where they originated.

[13] Material from *Cambridgeshire Times* (12 November 1937, p. 6), 'Death of The Rev. F. C. Davidson'. There were two Primitive Methodist districts in East Anglia, such was the strength of the church in this area: Lynn and Cambridge, with 5,846 members in 1902, and Norwich, 6,747 members. *1902 PM Minutes of Conference*, held at Wesley House, Cambridge.

[14] Copies of the Agendas for these conferences, with my grandfather's name on them in his own handwriting, were recently found in the safe at Manea (his last circuit), where they had lain for more than 60 years since his death.

[15] *Who's Who in Methodism 1933*.

[16] Quotation from the Connexional obituary, 1937.

[17] James Davidson.

[18] Ernest Fisher came from Sedgeford, near Docking in Norfolk, where FCD's father, James Davidson, was stationed twice, the first time in 1895. Ernest's father was a Local Preacher and Circuit Steward. Ernest and FCD may well have known each other before they went to Manchester (see Diary n. 18).

[19] George Robert Brake (1879-1954) was at the college at the same time. He would have been in his first year when FCD and Ernest Fisher were in their second year. From 1932 to 1938 he was serving in the Peterborough Circuit. Born at Odcombe in Somerset, he entered the ministry in 1905 and served in the following circuits: Docking (twice), Abertillery, Lydbrook, Oldham, Watton, Downham Market, Peterborough and Swindon. He then

31

retired to Sheringham in Norfolk. He was said to have worked with amazing energy and to have had a passion for preaching the gospel, such that he was preaching with vigour the day before he died. He also had a concern for Methodist property and in retirement he achieved the building of the Willie Long Memorial Chapel at West Runton. *Minutes of Conference 1955,* p.124; Leary, *Primitive Methodist Ministers.*

[20] John Norton (1880-1967) was a student at the college. He was born at Mattishall, Norfolk, and educated at East Dereham. After training at Hartley, he left in 1904 to go into circuit in Leicester and served in twelve more circuits, Balham, Wells, Sheringham, Derby III, Martham, Wangford, Barton on Humber, Brigg, Bury St. Edmunds, Petersfield, Frome and Llanymynech before retiring to Felixstowe in 1945, but later moved to Barton-on-Humber, where he spent his last thirteen years. He served faithfully throughout his life, continuing to preach until he was eighty. Leary, *Primitive Methodist Ministers; Minutes of Conference 1968.*

[21] See reference on Sunday 28 September in Diary.

[22] Frederick George Starling (1877-1944) was born at Swaffham in Norfolk. It appears he did not go to college, but went straight into circuit at Thetford in 1902. He then served in the following circuits: Crowle, Brigg, Winterton, Thetford, Grantham, Goole, Coventry, Nottingham Blue B, Nottingham West and Long Eaton, before retiring, through ill-health, to Long Eaton in 1941. *Minutes of Conference 1944,* p.143; Leary, *Primitive Methodist Ministers.*

[23] Frank Collen (1882-1942) was born at Soham Fen, trained at Hartley for three years and went into circuit in 1909 in Coventry. He then served in the following circuits: Coventry II, Watford, Bradford II, Coventry II, Hinkley, Leeds Meanwood and Church Gresley. As a preacher he was said to be stimulating, enriching and encouraging; as a pastor he had the sympathetic understanding to be able to guide and comfort his people and in administration he was painstaking and thorough. He died unexpectedly in 1942. *Minutes of Conference* 1943, p.121; Leary, *Primitive Methodist Ministers.*

[24] Milburn, *Primitive Methodism,* p. 82; Geoffrey Milburn and Margaret Batty (eds), *Workaday Preachers: the Story of Methodist Local Preaching* (Peterborough: Methodist Publishing House, 1995), p. 63.

[25] D. W. Bebbington, *The Nonconformist Conscience* (London: George Allen and Unwin, 1982), p. 4.

[26] Geoffrey Milburn, *Primitive Methodism,* p. 88.

[27] See A. L. Humphries, 'Hartley Primitive Methodist College', in W. Bardsley Brash, *The Story of Our Colleges 1835-1935* (London: Epworth Press, 1935), pp. 123-32.

[28] This would work out at just under 10 shillings a week during term-time, and would include tuition, heating and laundry. In 1900 Seebohm Rowntree made a study of families in York in which he concluded that the cost of food for a week for a man would be 3s 3d, for a woman 2s 9d and for children 2s 7d (older) to 2s 1d (younger) (John Burnett, *A History of the Cost of Living*, Harmondsworth: Penguin Books, 1954). £15 in 1876 has been calculated to be equivalent to £1,210 in October 2014; website: www.moneysorter.co.uk, [accessed on 17.10.14].

[29] Minutes, held at JRUL, of the PM Sunderland Institute Committee meeting, which took place on 25 August 1876.

[30] The college was constructed on the west side of Alexandra Road, between Brantingham Road and Gowan Road, nearly two miles south of the city centre and a short distance south of Alexandra Park, which is on the opposite side of the road. In its early days the college looked out on fields, but now a large area of suburban housing surrounds it. The building today is occupied by the Kassim Darwish Grammar School, an independent Muslim school for boys.

[31] The drawings and photographs referred to are held at the John Rylands University Library in Manchester.

[32] Examination of the accounts of Hartley College, held at the John Rylands Library, suggests that each student paid £7 10s every six months, i.e. £15 per year, but according to A. L. Humphries, the amount was £30 a year. However, the figure of £15 is confirmed by the Consolidated Rules of the 1902 PM Conference (see Appendix 2) and the College accounts, held at JRUL. This is in the context of the average working class household income in 1900 being estimated at 43 shillings (£2 3s) per week. The cost of food can be seen from an example of a clerk, with a wife and three children, earning 35s a week in 1904, who, over a 13 week period spent £12 6s 7d on food. A. L. Humphries, 'Hartley Primitive Methodist College', in Brash, *The Story of our Colleges*, p. 128; James Foreman-Peck (ed.), *New Perspectives on the Late Victorian Economy* (Cambridge: Cambridge University Press, 1991), pp. 158-9; Burnett, *A History of the Cost of Living*, pp. 271-2.

[33] William Pickles Hartley (1846-1922) was born in Colne, Lancashire, and rose from comparatively humble beginnings to create one of the largest preserves firms in the world, with purpose-built factories in Liverpool and London. Brought up in a Primitive Methodist family, his uncle was a

33

minister and his father a Local Preacher. He absorbed the values of thrift, hard work and a belief in the innate goodness of human beings. As his business grew, he used his wealth and influence to advance many philanthropic causes, which included hospitals and other public buildings, as well as a model village for his workers, and the Primitive Methodist Connexion was a particular beneficiary. His generosity set the Manchester College on a firm financial footing and enabled extensive building work, while his influence was instrumental in the recruitment of A. S. Peake. He was Vice-President of the PM Conference in 1892, President in 1909 and knighted for his public services in 1908. G. E. Milburn, in *Dictionary of Methodism* p. 151; Nicholas Hartley, *Bittersweet: The Story of Hartley's Jam* (Stroud: Amberley Publishing, 2011).

[34] See pp. 15-18, for further biographical information about A. S. Peake.

[35] The Hartley Collection at the John Rylands Library in Manchester contains a letter dated 6 July 1905 from the Registrar of the University of Manchester, Edward Fiddes, to 'The Principal of the Primitive Methodist College' stating that the Council has recognised the Primitive Methodist College in connection with the Faculty of Theology and that certain courses have been recognised. These are: A. S. Peake – Old Testament Introduction, New Testament Introduction and Old Testament Exegesis, and Rev. A. L. Humphries – New Testament Exegesis.

[36] Material drawn from papers for the year 1883 held at the John Rylands Library, Manchester.

[37] An example of an assignment was: 'Give a brief sketch of the progress of the Nation during the Plantagenet and Yorkist periods.'

[38] Questions such as: 'What is Conscience? How does Conscience express itself? In what does the authority of Conscience lie?' or 'Slavery stands condemned by what considerations? How does Wayland meet the objection that the Scriptures do not forbid slavery but tacitly allow it?'

[39] 'Name the foreign possessions of France,' was one question.

[40] Leslie S. Peake, *Arthur Samuel Peake, a Memoir* (London: Hodder and Stoughton, 1930), p. 103.

[41] *Minutes of Conference 1933*; John A. Vickers (ed.), *A Dictionary of Methodism in Britain and Ireland* (Peterborough: Epworth Press, 2000); Leary, *Primitive Methodist Ministers*.

[42] Biographical material obtained from the obituary by Rev. J. G. Bowran in the *PM Magazine 1919*, p. 702.

[43] 1851 Census.

[44] Leary, *Primitive Methodist Ministers*.

45 Material for this section is drawn from the following: Peake, *Arthur Samuel Peake*; John T. Wilkinson, *Arthur Samuel Peake* (London: Epworth Press, 1971); Martin Wellings, 'Arthur Samuel Peake', *BDE*, pp. 512-4; Vickers (ed.), *A Dictionary of Methodism in Britain and Ireland*.

46 W. F. Howard, quoted by Wellings, 'Arthur Samuel Peake'.

47 Samuel Peake served in the following circuits: Whitchurch, Cwm, Minsterley, Leominster, Leek, Hadnall, Bromsgrove, Church Stretton (twice), Stratford, Coventry, Peaton Road, Presteign, Liskeard, Ludlow, Birmingham and Ludlow, where he retired in 1896. Leary, *Primitive Methodist Ministers*.

48 Peake, *Arthur Samuel Peake*, p. 27.

49 Ibid. p. 50.

50 He remembered particularly C. K. Cheyne, the Oriel Professor, Samuel R. Driver, the Regius Professor of Hebrew and William Sanday, the Lady Margaret Professor of Divinity, who was not only a teacher, but a personal friend. He also appreciated the liberal intellect of Edwin Hatch, Reader in Ecclesiastical History.

51 D. Herridge, son of a Primitive Methodist minister, William G. Torr, a fellow-member of the Bible-reading class at St. John's, and Rev. E. R. Buckley, later Rector of Colchester, are mentioned by Wilkinson, *Arthur Samuel Peake*, pp. 40-42.

52 *The Bitter Cry of Outcast London*, which described the wretchedness of life in the slums of London, had a powerful influence on him. This was a revelatory and profoundly disturbing report produced by Andrew Mearns (1837-1925), a Congregationalist minster, born in Ayrshire. His overall focus was upon the physical and moral condition of London's slums, not least overcrowding and its consequences, sensationally numbering incest among the latter. The pamphlet came to the attention of W. T. Stead, the journalist and editor of the controversial *Pall Mall Gazette*, whose promotion of the work compounded the extraordinary response to its content. The furore prompted the churches to establish missions in the East End and in other cities, in an attempt to alleviate the misery Mearns described. BBC Website: London – Urban Explorers and Commentators, www.bbk.ac.uk/deviance/london/Mearns/index.htm [accessed 23.02.15].

53 Leslie Sillman Peake, MA BLitt (1900-84) studied at Mansfield College, Oxford and, entering the PM ministry in 1922, served in the following circuits: Middlesbrough I, Birmingham V, Preston, Penrith, Edinburgh (Nicholson Square), Falkirk, St. Ives and Wye Valley Mission, before retiring to Tewkesbury. He was known for his careful study, meticulous

preparation and ardent love of preaching, as well as his interest in literature and his care and understanding of people. Leary, *Primitive Methodist Ministers*; *Minutes of Conference 1985*.

[54] See Introduction n. 33 on William Pickles Hartley.

[55] He represented the faculty on the University senate from 1904 until his death and was Pro-Vice-Chancellor of the university in 1925. His achievements were recognised by honorary DD degrees from the universities of Aberdeen in 1907 and Oxford in 1920.

[56] This was followed by *Colossians* (1903), *The Problem of Suffering in the Old Testament* (1904), *Job* (1905), *A Critical Introduction to the New Testament* (1909), *Lamentations* (1912), *The Bible: Its Origin, Its Significance and Its Abiding Worth* (1913), *The Revelation of John* (1916) and *The Nature of Scripture* (1922).

[57] Peake, *Arthur Samuel Peake*, p. 294.

[58] *A Dictionary of Methodism in Britain and Ireland*, p. 268.

[59] His wide experience of the different denominations and his ecumenical outlook led to him serving as president of the National Council of the Evangelical Free Churches in 1928. He represented the Primitive Methodist Church on the Methodist Union Committee from 1918, meeting with the Anglicans at Lambeth Palace during the years 1922-5, and attending the Lausanne meeting of Faith and Order in 1927. He was also involved in the talks towards re-union of the Primitive, Wesleyan and United Methodist connexions and took part in drafting and amending the scheme and shaping the proposed doctrinal basis of the united church. Although he witnessed the vote in favour in 1928, sadly he did not live to attend the Uniting Conference of 1932.

[60] Held at John Rylands Library, Manchester.

[61] Ill health remained a problem for him, although he continued to undertake a prodigious amount of work, and from 1912 his days were lengthened by having to make the journey to Freshfield on the coast, since the family had moved there on account of the boys' health. Eight years later the family was able to move back to Manchester, but over the years he continued to suffer from the hyatid cysts on the liver which were to necessitate a second operation.

[62] John T. Wilkinson, *Arthur Samuel Peake*, p. 43.

[63] *Minutes of Conference 1950*.

[64] *Who's Who in Methodism 1933*.

[65] Biographical material is from the *PM Magazine 1906*, p. 242.

[66] William George Softley (1870-1949), who was born at East Walton, King's Lynn. After lay appointments in Norfolk, Kent and Wales, he entered the Manchester PM College in 1897. His first appointment in 1899 was at Wrockwardine Wood. He then served in the following circuits: Hasbury, Spalding, Manea, Leeds X, Fakenham, Peterborough I, Newark (or possibly Newmarket – see Minutes of Conference), Kingstone and Weardale. He was fond of music and formed music classes in many of his circuits and revived village causes. He retired in 1939 to Ingoldisthorpe, near his King's Lynn home. He was very possibly already known to FCD from the days before he went to college. *Minutes of Conference 1949;* Leary, *Primitive Methodist Ministers* (see Diary n. 299, Sunday 23 November).

[67] Held at the John Rylands Library, Manchester.

[68] Advertisement for Saunders & Taylor of Manchester in the *PM Minutes of Conference 1902.*

[69] Further details of the syllabus and examination questions are to be found in the Appendices.

[70] Taken from 2 Cor 3:17b (in the Latin Vulgate translation).

[71] Victoria Park College opened in Manchester in 1871 to train United Methodist Free Church ministers. After the union of 1907 with the Methodist New Connexion and the Bible Christians to form the United Methodist Church, Victoria Park provided for second and third year students and Ranmoor College in Sheffield for first years. *Dictionary of Methodism,* p. 364.

[72] See comment in the Diary for 13 August on the Owens College buildings (Diary n. 31).

[73] B. R. Mitchell, *British Historical Statistics* (Cambridge: Cambridge University Press, 1988), pp. 330-4.

[74] Jonathan Schofield, *Manchester Then and Now* (London: Batsford, 2009).

[75] *Building News,* 1861, quoted by Cecil Steward, *The Stones of Manchester* (London: Edward Arnold Publishers Ltd, 1956), on which this whole section draws.

[76] See Schofield, *Manchester Then and Now,* pp. 56-7.

[77] John H. G. Archer, 'A Classic of its Age', and Julian Treuherz, 'Ford Madox Brown and the Manchester Murals', in John H. G. Archer (ed.), *Art and Architecture in Victorian Manchester* (Manchester: Manchester University Press, 1985), pp. 127-161, 162-83 (see Diary n. 22 for a fuller description of the Town Hall).

[78] Treuherz, 'Ford Madox Brown and the Manchester murals'. See also reference to Ford Madox Brown in Diary n. 60 on 25 August.

[79] Stuart Hylton, *A History of Manchester* (Andover: Phillimore, 2010), pp. 161-2 (see further Diary n. 31 on Owens College).

[80] This section draws on D. W. Bebbington, *The Nonconformist Conscience* (London: George Allen and Unwin, 1982), ch. 7; G. I. T. Machin, *Politics and Churches in Great Britain 1869-1921* (Oxford: Clarendon Press, 1987), pp. 225-30, 260-73; James Munson, *The Nonconformists* (London: SPCK, 1991), ch. 9; Edward Royle, *Modern Britain: A Social History 1750-2011*, 3rd ed. (London: Bloomsbury, 2012).

[81] C. H. Kelly, speaking to the Free Church National Council Conference against the Education Act, April 1902, cited by Bebbington, *The Nonconformist Conscience*, chapter 7.

[82] See Munson, *The Nonconformists,* pp. 247-63.

[83] Machin, *Politics and the Churches in Great Britain,* pp. 228-9.

[84] Royle, *Modern Britain: A Social History,* p. 414.

[85] Machin, *Politics and Churches in Great Britain,* p. 262.

[86] *British Weekly* 10 June 1901, cited by Bebbington, *The Nonconformist Conscience,* p. 142.

[87] The number was 60, up to February 1907, compared with 48 Baptists, 40 Congregationalists, 15 Wesleyans and 27 others. Machin, *Politics and Churches in Great Britain 1869-1921*, p. 267.

THE DIARY

Monday 4 August 1902[1]
Journeyed to Manchester. Started from Stow Bedon[2] at 10.6 and arrived in Lynn[3] at 11.17. Went up into town and called to see one or two friends. Left Lynn 12.12 and ultimately arrived at Lincoln.[4] The city has a very pleasant aspect from the line.[5] The cathedral[6] on summit of hill and red brick houses on side of the hill. The walk from station to cathedral is very wearying indeed. For nearly 100 yards the road is exceptionally steep. The road from Staithes (Yorkshire) to the station is about the only steep incline to be compared with the above (that I have climbed). After much labouring arrived at the top and went into cathedral and had a look round. It is a beautiful structure, fine art work and decorations. The chancel appears, as seen through the gates,[7] to be even more beautiful. There is much display of art on the outside of the building, with the two towers at one end and the one over the centre of the building. The sight amply repaid for the tedious walk necessary beforehand.

From Lincoln got a through carriage to Manchester.[8] No special scenery to Sheffield, but after leaving the scenery was simply grand. Hills and dales thickly covered with trees, and water rolling down inclines.[9] Passed through one tunnel nearly 4 miles long. Then into London Rd.[10] about ¼ to seven,[11] and arrived safely at College, which is a very fine building.[12] General structure is that of 3 sides of a rectangle. One wing, 3 storeys, all studies, 20 along each of the three corridors, and bedrooms arranged similarly, 2 wings connected with 3 long passages. On the 1st floor Dining Room, Governor's or Tutor's Rooms. Library, Kitchen etc., Assembly Room 2nd Floor.

Wednesday 6 August
Principal Parkin[13] met us and introduced Professor Humphries[14] recently appointed as Greek Professor. Professor Peake[15] met us and outlined his work. Rather short, busy, not an orator.[16]
Even had a 'Camp Meeting'[17] sustained by 2nd Years in my Study and left all in darkness. Disturbed in the night by would-be visitors, but key was turned against them.

Thursday 7 August
A hard morning. 4 hours almost continuous writing lectures. One from Mr Parkin, three from Prof. Peake.

Friday 8 August
Had just a few letters in Hebrew language given by Mr Parkin. Afternoon: Annual Meeting, and at dinner it was announced that if students wanted linen collected to put them out. When all busy, in marched two with dirty linen and night shirts: during meeting Governor came in, just cast his eyes and smiled. During meeting there was what was termed a Christening Meeting as nicknames were given. Mine was Absalom and, seeing I am Davids(s)on, it was very appropriate. One who has 3 or 4 Christian names was called Legion. Fisher[18] (Shrimp). Dawson[19] (Gill).

Saturday 9 August
Coronation Day[20] and I was thankful to God who had spared me to see that day, which celebrated my nineteenth birthday. Some Japanese fireworks[21] were sent up in Alexandra Park. After the noise of the explosion, a ball was seen in the air which exploded and then various animals floated about. In evening went into the city. Town Hall.[22] Exchange.[23] Many people promenading to see an electric car[24] profusely illuminated by various coloured bulb lamps.[25]

Sunday 10 August
Planned[26] and went to Brookbottom.[27] Travelled through beautiful scenery. Saw The Peak in the distance and a river rising on side. Spoke in school in morning. Preached in afternoon and evening. Did not feel as free as could have wished; enjoyed service in evening and congregation seemed to also. Arrived back 10.30. Surprised to see so much Sunday traffic: trippers etc. The hills were very lofty and a beautiful valley lay between.

Monday 11 August
In afternoon went for a walk and had a look round a small art gallery, nothing special. Walked through Whitworth Park,[28] a fine stretch of grounds. Passed Rev. A. Maclaren's[29] church,[30] rather deceived when saw the size from outward appearances; nothing out of the common.

Tuesday 12 August
Lectures in morning. In afternoon Cricket Match, 2nd v. 1st years. 2nd
years won easily. I was rather unfortunate to get bowled, off my legs.
'Off my pads' would be more scientific language, but I had no pads on.

Wednesday 13 August
In afternoon went via Whitworth Park to Owen's College Museum.[31]
The college itself appears a fine building, a new wing has lately been
added, a contrast between the new stone and the old, blackened by
course of long years.[32]
A fine Museum, splendid collections of minerals (one thing of interest
was the brilliant mock diamond, with card saying purchased for
enormous sum. I called attention of E.F.[33] to it but then noticed words
'Model of Diamond.' not the reality, the model). Splendid collection of
beasts and birds and reptiles, birds of most gorgeous and dazzling hues.
An Egyptian mummy was also seen.

Thursday 14 August
In afternoon went to Whitworth Art Gallery.[34] A fine institution,
magnificent collection of paintings, drawings, statues. The paintings
were almost enough to dazzle one. On 2nd floor, fine specimens of
work done in past ages, also of present time in foreign countries,
magnificent robes. There was some beautiful work in beads. One had to
look closely to see the beads, which were of different colours and
worked into pretty designs.

Friday 15 August
In morning met the Principal who gave a very interesting talk on
Theology and made it clear that we must not despise certain Non-
Christian Religions. Buddhism and Islam.[35] He said he believed the
founder of the former was or is with Jesus.[36]
In evening assembled in Library to listen to a concert. The room
presented a very pleasing aspect, students making themselves quite at
home on lounge chairs. The concert was one of class. Some splendid
talent was exhibited. In vocal and instrumental music, two violin solos
were quite a credit to the musician, Mr Wightman.[37] A splendid
recitation from Henry VIII was given by Mr Hooson,[38] the best actor
I have seen. If so inclined, he should have no difficulty in securing
a prominent place on the stage. God grant he may never be so inclined.

Saturday 16 August

Met Mr Parkin, who gave us some friendly and valuable advice as to matters to be observed when in company (pulpit and indoors). In afternoon went to Moseley St. Art Gallery.[39] The finest collection of paintings I have ever seen, simply grand: masterpieces of some of most noted artists. (Oh what a daub and mess they look to be when viewed from short distance, but how beautiful when viewed from the distance).

Sunday 17 August

Went to Withington Camp Meeting;[40] about 17 of the students went, a grand little army. Prayer Meeting in morning, then House to House Visitation. E.E.F.[41] and I were posted on main road opposite a large Public House to distribute bills. Not a very comfortable duty, but it was for advancing Christ's Kingdom. Some silk hats passed by with a haughty air while poor people accepted. It was painful to see (as far as could be seen) the little effect the announcements on the bill had. God grant time may speedily come when publics will be closed on Sundays (at least) and those who frequent such places now may attend God's House!

Dined with a Mrs Wright: splendid home: welcome and hearty reception, felt rather strange at first. In afternoon, owing to wet, had service in chapel; 3 students spoke very well.

Had tea with Host. Another member of family made an appearance at tea table; enjoyable time.

In evening two students spoke; enjoyed the discourses; felt God present and working upon the hearts of some. A good prayer meeting but no visible signs of any gaining victory over sin. A young woman was convicted but passed out without coming to penitent form. When I retired to rest I wondered about that young woman. When out in streets, possibly met by some friends, hallowed influence becomes dispersed ...

Went to supper with Mr W.[42] Felt more at home. Miss W. played and another young gentleman played violin. Enjoyed music very much. After prayers returned back to college.

Monday 18 August

In afternoon went into city to Cathedral.[43] Went past without knowing it was the cathedral, a very small building from outward appearances, with simply one square tower. Inside very acceptable, nothing to boast of. Rode back on a tram from Exchange station.[44] Passed Lewis's.[45] A fine shop. Much traffic about.

Tuesday 19 August

In evening a reception was given by Great Western Street Church[46] to students. A bountiful tea was provided free to students. A platform meeting was held afterwards. Rev. Neilson MA BD[47], took chair, and gave a hearty welcome to students. Mr Kinnish (2nd year)[48] and Mr Cook [sic] (1st year)[49] replied. Rev. Humphries MA, Rev. Parkin MA BD (Principal), and Prof. Peake all spoke; a very enjoyable evening was spent.

Wednesday 20 August

In afternoon another cricket match was played. 2nd v. 1st years. 2nd years made about 100. Splendid catches were made by Palmer[50], Hill[51] (who caught two) and myself (I apologize for personal reference). Our year made about 49; I had the good fortune to make 23 not out. Next highest scores were 5 and 5. I was carried off the field, shoulder high.

Several 1st year men have been 'had up' at dinner table for various charges: e.g. 'getting their hair cut without permission of a 2nd year man', 'for being seen out with a young lady (sisters or friends)'. They have been called upon to explain such conduct. Much fun is forthcoming from such incidents.

Thursday 21 August

A hard day: lectures and getting declensions up, also Hebrew. In the evening at supper table a 2nd year man got up to propose a severe censure should be passed on a 1st year man 'for showing such a face' (he had had his moustache shaved off). Another 2nd year man got up and spoke of the seriousness of the offence and seconded the motion; another 2nd year supported. Now the greatest amusement prevailed for each of these 2nd year men had been guilty of the same offence, hence the joke. In reply the 1st year man said he thought they had all been tarred with the same stick. One of the above got up and thought it would be better to say 'lathered with the same brush' (laughter).

Friday 22 August

Been a high time this afternoon. Bills had been printed announcing 'a special treat' in a lecture by the 'Baby' of the 1st year on 'Palmistry'.

The individual has already had too much to say – a bore – and had bragged about it undoubtedly. Chair taken by Mr 'Custard' K..[52] Before lecture commenced a quartet was rendered by the members of the 'bare-faced boys brigade' mentioned above, dressed with high collars, waistcoats up to collars, black straw hats and a pink flower in each coat. Their voices blended nicely when they could keep from laughing. Of course the chairman introduced the lecturer in the usual way and a great ovation was given him (waving handkerchiefs etc.). The lecture was interspersed with bursts of applause and he demonstrated practically on three hands (some hands were previously marked with pencil etc.). When the lecture was over the usual votes of thanks were passed and a presentation made for his services, a piece of plate and an illuminated address (a broken plate, a piece of candle lighted on card board). He braved it out well. A meeting was held afterwards and it was decided to confer a degree upon him with certificate, cap and gown.

Early on Saturday morning were disturbed by singing along our corridor. 'There are angels hovering around,' the harmony was very good, but scarcely the time to be singing and rattling doors.

Saturday 23 August
Nothing special, only two more caught the fever for shaving; one with heavy dark moustache looked quite different when shaved.

Just at close of class Mr Parkin said he would not say much more. Someone called out 'Hear, Hear.' The Principal smiled and said, 'One must not always pay heed to what people say, and told the following incident: When leaving one of his circuits he was preaching at one place for the last time but did not preach a farewell sermon; before closing he said that would be the last time, he expected, and would like to shake hands with the people before leaving. One of the most prominent men immediately struck up 'Praise God from whom all blessings flow'! Mr Parkin added 'I knew the man.'

Sunday 24 August
Short prayer meeting after breakfast. Some astir early to catch trains. In morning went to Great Western Street Chapel, a very nice chapel, rather spiff. Good organ with beautiful picillo[53] stop. A first-year man preached; good sermon; not many people; singing by no means perfect. Afternoon went to PSA[54] held in an adjoining hall. Nice company; two good solos were rendered.

Band in Park,[55] thousands of people.
Evening went to Union Chapel (Dr Maclaren's),[56] Rev. Roberts MA
BD[57] preached from Revelation 7:14-15, Heaven is not so far off as we
expect or think. Heaven is being with God, so in minor degree earth can
be Heaven. He did not think the babe enters the same heaven as the
aged Christian, nor thief as suffering saint. Earth a school for
development which will be carried over and continued in Heaven.
It is a fine Church, not to be compared with City Temple. Perhaps seats
2,000. Organ, nothing extra; choir small but good, not up to
expectations. I was struck with simplicity of service; no voluntaries;
preacher alone repeated Lord's Prayer; no vesper, only the usual psalm.
Preacher seemed at a loss for words once or twice.

Monday 25 August
Went to Moseley Street Art Gallery[58] again: 'The Shadow of the
Cross,'[59] 'Work'[60] and many other grand paintings.

Tuesday 26 August
Another hard morning. Prof. Peake made us skip along. In evening
Principal Parkin preached. Rev. 21:5, 'Behold I make all things new.'
New individual, new world, new church, new service.
Well off – had three letters and a parcel.

Wednesday 27 August
Wet afternoon.

Thursday 28 August
In afternoon went shopping. Walked right up into city. Lewis's[61] is a
fine shop. I went to Paulden's,[62] a fine shop, wonderful; felt rather
awkward 'shopping', not in my line.

Friday 29 August
In afternoon a debate on 'Is smoking a pernicious habit?' Very good
meeting; much said in favour of both sides. Non-smokers obtained
majority of votes.

Saturday 30 August
Mr Parkin had some plain conversation with us in the morning. In
afternoon preparing for Blackburn.[63] Train was due out of Victoria

6.30, but was very late and did not start until 7.20.[64] Many excursionists about for Blackpool. We did spin along most of the way, especially through a tunnel we appeared to be flying. Without much difficulty found my home in 42 Granville Road,[65] Mr Jos. Hindle.[66] A fine home. Mr and Mrs were at business, but Miss H. prepared supper. Retired about 10, but did not have a good night's rest – thoughts of the Sunday.

Sunday 31 August

Met Mr and Mrs H.; very nice people. Had a 2 miles walk to Chapel (Oxford Street),[67] a fine place, not quite as large as London Road, Lynn;[68] quite an experience for me. Long order of service. Did not feel as bad as I expected, not a large company. In afternoon went over to Princes' Street School (Day and Sunday)[69] and took tea with Mr and Mrs and Miss Bolton,[70] quite singular that I should meet with them. In evening again spoke at Oxford Street; had a fairly good time. Nice company of young people in Gallery, not many below. Splendid choir for the number present. Several young people stayed to prayer meeting, not one of the best for 'Go'.[71]

Monday 1 September

Morning: had breakfast alone; others off to business. Journeyed to Manchester by 9.35 from Blackburn; train late; did go some parts of journey.

In evening CE[72] meeting. Mr Parkin conducted. Rev. Humphries gave a very good address.

Tuesday 2 September

Monotonous morning working in a stuffy Lecture Hall. In afternoon a great event happened, viz. presentation of cap, gown, certificate and medal to the lecturer on Palmistry. A surplice (nightshirts) was in attendance, with candles. Addresses given in the presentation of the various honours. Much mirth was caused. The lecturer took all without resistance. Specially composed songs and quartets rendered by boys of bare face brigade.

In evening a preaching service. Mr Bishell[73] preached very nicely from Psalms 17:15.

In night disturbed by doors banging.

Wednesday 3 September
Had a game of football in afternoon.

Thursday 4 September
Have been into city this afternoon. Went into the market.[74] Much garden produce was there. On way saw some immense buildings (Technical School,[75] warehouses,[76] Police Courts[77] etc.).

Saturday 6 September
Morning: Criticism class on above sermon. Several testified to benefit and help received from sermon.
Went into market; much provision and produce on view. Went into 'penny stores'; wonderful the articles for one penny. In evening had a surprise visit from C. Wright.[78] Received Gladstone bag as a present from Fincham.[79]

Sunday 7 September
Morning: went to Chorlton Road Chapel.[80] Dr. Gooderich, [sic][81] a noted preacher. Text: 'Do this in remembrance of me.'[82] Good sermon; not appearance of 'great sermon'. Fine church; good choir and organ.
Afternoon: went to Withington. Bible Class. W. Farndale[83] gave address. Had tea with Mr Wright, also supper; enjoyable time. Evening a superannuated minister preached.

Monday 8 September
Afternoon: went to Owen's [sic] College Museum; fine collection of birds and animals. An accident on football field – a 2nd year man fell and broke his wrist. In evening a sacramental service. Wrote a letter of thanks to Fincham for bag.

Tuesday 9 September
In afternoon went and heard Rev. F. B. Meyer BA.[84] He gave a short address upon the barren fig tree [Matthew 21:19-22]: 'If thou had faith ... mountain ... sea', speaking on removing mountains from our lives. Enjoyed him much, very spiritual and simple. It was a service in connection with his conferential tour to P.S. workers;[85] a short convention afterwards.
Student preached in evening for Criticism (Class).

47

Wednesday 10 September
Felt benefited by game of football.[86]

Thursday 11 September
Professor Peake away,[87] so no lectures, but a Hebrew Class, and Prof. Humphries met us respecting Latin.

Friday 12 September
Several beds turned over, one bed the clothes rolled quite up. Necessary utensils missing from rooms, found in bathroom. My bed alright.

Saturday 13 September
Morning: Principal Parkin referred to bed raiding and appealed to consciences and showed how more work was put on the maids,[88] which was unjust.
Criticism Class: preacher on Tuesday was very nervous so was excused some of the mistakes he made; the critique dealt very kindly with him.
Went in search of Charlie Mills, was not successful in finding him.
Afternoon: had a game of football. Evening: Mr N. from Blackburn came to see me.

Sunday 14 September
In morning went to Great Western Street. Nice congregation; good service. Rev. Neilson preached. 'Your life is hid – in God.'[89] Christian life is hidden (1) in its beginning (2) from world (3) from ourselves. Fine illustration – children chasing butterflies, leaving mother alone at tombstone.
Afternoon went to PSA.[90] Rev. N.[91] gave address on Culture, Physical, Intellectual and Spiritual. Two very good solos were rendered by a young soloist.
In evening went with Ernest[92] to Ridgeway Street, a mission.[93] I prayed and read lesson. Was very nervous. An open-air service was held afterwards; young women rallied well. I spoke; enjoyed the meeting.

Monday 15 September
Went to Moseley Street Art Gallery:[94] a new collection of paintings; fine art exhibition. Went in search of C. Mills; unfruitful search.

Tuesday 16 September
Evening: Mr Emmett[95] preached on 'Christian race'.

Wednesday 17 September
Wet afternoon; just went for a walk.

Friday 19 September
In evening had a splendid entertainment, consisting largely of recitations from a popular elocutionist (Mr Bernard).[96] He is a splendid reciter and gave us a variety, solemn, exciting, humorous. Among the former – The unfinished picture: an old painter painted a picture of Christ but left the face to be completed when he could paint one lovely, deep etc. He was dying and suddenly he jumped up saying, 'I have seen it – the face.' He called for his palette and brush, then with his hands he made marks as if finishing the picture – most impressive piece, most impressively rendered.
Another was about a slave who had worked in a gold field and gathered enough gold to purchase the ransom of his lover. He was proceeding there by ship. He had taken the invalid child of the captain ashore on an island and was surprised with savages. He plunged into the sea but was wounded. To save the child's life, he cut the leather belt containing the ransom and it sank but he saved the child's life. When dying, he said he was going to 'Olde Virginie'.
Humorous: variations on 'Mary had a little lamb', 'The Water Wheel', 'Little Bill.' It was quite an enjoyable evening. One student stayed in his study to 'swot' to the disgust of other students.

Saturday 20 September
Criticism Class; and Mr Parkin showed us how to use the fire appliances. In afternoon went to 'Belle Vue'.[97] Somewhat sorry that Mr Chesworth[98] and I had made arrangements, for there were Chapel opening services at Chorlton.[99] The President, Rev. Mitchell,[100] was present.
We trained[101] and had just a nice walk to Gardens. It is truly a wonderful place for pleasure. There is a fine menagerie. We saw two lions fed; their instinct seemed to tell them it was time to be fed, for they very impatiently walked backwards and forwards past the door where the keeper came in. We saw various wild animals: a huge hippopotamus which opened its massive mouth showing its 'grinders' for biscuits to be thrown into it. An elephant would put a penny into

49

a slot and walk round then come to get the biscuit that had fallen out of the machine; it would ring a bell when asked. There was a monkey which did a similar thing to obtain a nut. We saw some snakes; one python 27 feet long, massive creature, also another very thick snake. Tea is very expensive there (best to take something to eat; hot water can be obtained). Teas 1/- each; one cup 3d.[102] Went into cinematograph show. Saw some good scenes including Coronation Procession. Went into the 'Maze' and had a difficult task to get to the centre, not so bad coming back.

The Monkey house is very interesting – all sizes, shapes etc. One smaller monkey was very busy seeking for 'something' or 'somethings' in the coat of a larger monkey which seemed to enjoy being searched! So natural. We saw a chimpanzee – most human looking creature, many actions like a human being; it had a looking glass; except for the vacant look it had a human appearance. Fine collection of birds in a large cage. Fine imitation of 'sea on land'.

Towards evening there was dancing, some bad life carried on there. The whole afternoon was crowned with fireworks. Huge scene representing South Africa and this was illuminated and was the scene of a sham fight, Britons v. Boers.[103] A wonderful sight. We saw the surrender of Cronje.[104] There were rockets and other gorgeous fireworks – a grand display. An illuminated representation of King in the Stage Coach drawn by horses. I think the whole concern can be well spoken of as 'Vanity Fair'.[105] Still it is worth seeing. But 'be careful' 'oh be careful'.[106] Took electric tram back into city.

Sunday 21 September
In morning went to Union Chapel and heard Dr Maclaren. A fine congregation and good service. A very deep but splendid sermon, but cannot remember much of it as a sermon i.e. of 'outline'.

He gave some fine illustrations: 'Black Book', 'Mountain Ash in sunshine', 'Tree in thicket', 'Grape vine in cold country'.

In afternoon went to great Western Street PSA.[107] The chapel was decorated nicely.

In evening preached at Monmouth Street, Rusholme.[108] Fairly good service; not quite such a good time as I had expected.

Monday 22 September
Received Lynn News[109] from M. Walsh.[110]

Tuesday 23 September
Received few flowers[111] and letter from home. Preaching service. 'Let us come boldly etc.'[112] Enjoyed the service. (Mr Evans).[113]

Wednesday 24 September
The years' match. I had the honour to play; did not do great things. Our team played well – the goal-keeper (Mr Cook)[114] splendidly. The 1st years lost 0-1.

Thursday 25 September
The 'no-goods' match. This caused the greatest fun imaginable. Several had scarcely kicked a football. To see these rigged up in football costume was a grand sight, and to see them on the field, running all over, 'beating the air' as E. Fisher[115] said in a speech, and kicking through their own goal. Poor fellows, some were stiff next morn!

Saturday 27 September
Went to see C. Mills. Met him at his office and went to Free Trade Hall[116] and saw 'Hamilton's tour round the world.'[117] These were splendidly painted pictures, illuminated from behind, of various places and scenes round the world. In some cases they obtained a moving effect[118] (steamer going out of harbour). These were interspersed with Living pictures (Coronation Procession,[119] Preston Guild,[120] Welcome to Kitchener[121]). A wonderful display was given by two acrobats. A Chinaman also gave a fine display of conjuring; he did some wonderful tricks: eating fire and cotton wool and made smoke and flames issue from his mouth. He put a flower (in bloom) into an empty flower-pot etc. etc. There were various other small entertainments. Went to tea with Charlie. Enjoyed myself much. He showed me his tunic and rifle.
(One student was prevailed upon to write an essay upon Love, courtship and marriage, as he had bought a book on the subject. He almost finished it when he found out it was a joke. He tore it up but others got the pieces and pasted them together. It was read and caused much amusement.)

Sunday 28 September
Went to Western Street in morning and heard Mr Norton[122] preach from 'Apart from Me, ye can do nothing'.[123] Nice short service.

In afternoon went to PSA.[124] A Missioner to Police Courts[125] gave a thrilling address on his work among criminals and said how he had come to the conclusion that 90% of crime was due to 'Indifference,' hence drinking – bad company – gambling. One lad at 18 sentenced to 3 years for house-breaking[126] and said he wish it had been 30 years – tired of life. One touching incident of young man repenting just before being hanged. Kissed the missioner and told him to take it to his mother. In evening went and heard Dr Forsyth (Hackney College)[127] at Dr Gooderich's [sic] Church;[128] grand service; subject: 'Young man's Golden Ladder'. In faith add virtue, etc.

Monday 29 September
Evening: nice C.E.[129] address by Mr Hughes[130] on 'Influence'.

Tuesday 30 September
Went to a great Education Meeting[131] in Central Hall; fine meeting; splendid company. Dr Maclaren[132] Chairman, Dr Fairburn[133] [sic], Dr Moulton,[134] Rev. Townsend,[135] Dr McKennel[136] [sic] speakers. Supported by many other ministers etc.
(Some time ago a motion was passed that one student 'kaffir' should be the critique for the Governor's sermon. He went and asked for his MSS. The Governor looked at him, then laughed.)

Thursday 2 October
Had some serious business at dinner table respecting Praying in the Lecture Hall; to one (probably more) there did not seem to be an atmosphere congenial to Prayer, but it is not the place, not the company, it is the heart of the child of God. Such a case scarcely should have arisen.
Some thought that a levy of 9d[137] was rather inconsistent after previous levies; this levy was mainly due to athletic expenses.

Sunday 5 October
In morning went and heard Dr Maclaren. A very good service and splendid sermon. 'This do in remembrance of Me.'[138] (1) A glimpse into the heart of Jesus. (2) A barrier of sense obscuring this. (3) Christ's own witness to what he thought the centre of His work: This. (4) A solemn claim to our hearts to love and remembrance: 'Of Me'.

One or two fine passages: one about the little mound outside city wall rising above the horizon when highest peaks of Himalayas do grow less and less, and growing brighter and brighter as the ages recede, and the closing passage: the whole heaven behind filled with the light of that face which was crowned with thorns; the whole heaven before filled with the light of the face crowned with glory.

In afternoon, went to PSA. A good service. Went to Rev. Neilson's to tea and supper; enjoyed myself playing and singing. Went to Western Street in evening; had a good service. Mr Jones[139] preached.

In morning just before service commenced a fire was discovered below the chapel in connection with the heating apparatus. Fortunately extinguished without much damage.

Monday 6 October
Went to Withington in evening to fruit banquet.[140] Rev. Neilson gave a few selections from R. Burns[141]. We had solos, vocal and violin; recitation. Fruit passed round. Had an enjoyable evening. Saw the Wright family and had hearty invitation to go and see them again.

Tuesday 7 October
Had the good fortune to receive 3 letters: Lynn, Downham and Rockland. Quite cheered me up.
Nice preaching service. Mr Fairweather,[142] was very courageous

Wednesday 8 October
Had a splendid outing to Mr Beeley's.[143] Woodley[144] after getting off the train. Went for a walk up the hills, beautiful scenery, hill and dale; tall chimneys issuing out dense volumes of smoke, which mistified[145] the atmosphere could be seen far and near. Ultimately came to Mr Beeley's; a splendid home and grounds; for natural beauty they would be hard to be beaten, for included was a pretty dell, growing trees and thick undergrowth. Paths were on the hillside; it would be a lovely sight in summer. We feasted on some apples left on one tree (also on pears). We sat down to a splendid repast, one of the grandest outsets[146] I have seen – we did full justice (as will be seen as the maids at college said we couldn't have been hungry seeing we left so much (even cheese) at supper.[147] Mr Beeley appeared a nice, kind-hearted gentleman and said we must go again. He generously paid the train fare.

Thursday 9 October
A very wet day. How fortunate we were to have it fine yesterday.

Friday 10 October
I think it was Thursday evening when some went to bed they found
their beds occupied. It was quite a joke; the occupants were dolls made
out of nightshirts and pillows etc. with black pieces pinned for eyes etc.
E. E. Fisher[148] said he was startled when he first saw one in his bed.
Some of the 1st years went bed-raiding the 2nd years but were caught
and one poor little fellow (Brown)[149] had a hot time of it; was locked in
old Library but cleverly poured some water over 2nd year man. This
made persecution the more heated; quite a commotion along the
corridors in dark. The Governor came and there was a hush suddenly.

Saturday 11 October
A great demonstration against Education Bill.[150] Hundreds of people
congregated in Albert Square[151] and accompanied with bands and
banners marched to Alexandra Park. It was an immense procession.
I was in the middle and could not see the end; it took ¾ of an hour to
pass a certain point. In the Park there were stands, and thousands were
gathered. Several MPs were there. I heard Hutton Esq. MP,[152]
Broadhurst MP,[153] Rev. S. Chadwick,[154] Rev. Roberts.[155] At quarter
past 5 a Resolution was put simultaneously at the stands and carried
with acclamation. There was a small disturbance afterwards.

Sunday 12 October
In morning went to Great Western Street. Rev. Hind (York)[156] preached
– comparing old Covenant with the New. In afternoon went to PSA.
Rev. Hind spoke on an 'Ideal Man.' Preached at Booth St. Mission in
evening; small company, not very lively. Went to Rev. Neilson's to
supper. Met a Rev. Barber (Tunstall Circuit).[157] Enjoyed singing and
conversation; returned to college at very late hour.

Monday 13 October
Evening: went to Great Western Street Public Service. Rev. Hind gave
a good address in course of which he said long since he came to the
conclusion that any church could have a revival when it wanted.
He spoke of a great revival on one of his circuits without special
services. Conversions came every Sunday evening after service for

54

3 months. He went round one Sunday Evening in Prayer Meeting but out of 400 there were no sinners. He then asked if they were going to allow a break in Good Work. They then entered sincerely into Prayer and ere long 12 walked in and knelt at penitent (communion) rail. People who had been at services but had gone away. He said we must be definite in Prayer. Rev. Beavan[158] spoke on 'life' and Rev. Neilson [also spoke].

Tuesday 14 October

Two great meetings in Manchester. United Kingdom Alliance[159] and Mr Balfour (Premier).[160]
U.K.A. was held in Free Trade Hall: about 4,000 or more were there. A good meeting. Lord Provost of Glasgow presided. Sir William [*sic*] Lawson[161] (witty and humorous), Mr Jones M.A.,[162] Canon Hicks,[163] T. P. Whittaker M.P.,[164] W. Wightman L.C.C.[165] (formerly a schoolmaster – told some pitiful stories from self-observation and experience), Rev. Silas Hocking[166] and Rev. L. Isitt[167] were speakers. About £3,000[168] was promised at the Meeting; fine meeting. Mr Balfour[169] addressed about 7,000 in St. James' Hall.[170] Gave a long speech on Education Bill; said Non-conformists' grievances were exaggerated.

Wednesday 15 October

Went and had photos taken.[171] Had to sit in the light of several incandescent lamps with light thrown on the face by shade.

Thursday 16 October

Received photos. They are very nice, especially for the money. 1/3 per dozen.[172]

Friday 17 October

Worked morning and afternoon. In evening went to Withington. This was fine treat for us to get in room with cheering fire. Had music and ping-pong. I was quite taken up with the game and played very well, so I was told. We had a splendid supper and returned rather late.

Sunday 19 October

In morning went and heard Rev. Maclaren. Text: Psalms 99:8. (1) God's forgiveness (2) God's scourging (3) Forgiveness and scourging of Holy Love. A fine sermon and splendid service. (Matter is

55

put very similarly in Dr Clark.)[173] After service had a very pressing invitation to go down to Withington. In afternoon went to P.S.A.;[174] a very nice service. Two splendid solos, fairly well sung. A very unique address, full of dry humour. He talked of 'pawning himself and losing the ticket,' that in leaving or gathering riches for children, parents sometimes secure for them a first-class ticket to hell.

Went to W.[175] for tea. Another splendid tea; also enjoyed music and supper. (Went to chapel in evening).

Monday 20 October

We played another year's match. I thought we should be beaten but found we kept the 2nd years out better than expectation and ultimately won them 2-1. I scored one goal, which was termed 'a beautiful shot.'

Friday 24 October

In evening we had a concert, quite a fine one: recitations, exceptionally good violin solo, vocal solos, quartet and chorus; this, so we were told, was splendid, the parts blended well. I sang first bass.

Saturday 25 October

In evening went to Central Hall and heard M. G. Pearse[176] lecture on 'How I came to sign the pledge.' Hall crowded. Enjoyed it much; he told some touching stories.

Sunday 26 October

Morning and afternoon went to Western St. Rev. Neilson[177] preached in morning; nice service. In evening went to Free Trade Hall. I don't think I was in such a service before. 5-6 thousand people there. One sea of faces, and when rose to sing seemed one solid mass. Large choir and orchestra. I was enraptured and could not sing for some time; had to listen, then I tried to swell the mighty song. Rev. M. G. Pearse gave a very graphic address on Peter's Fall and Restoration. I have never seen picture (imaginary) drawn so vividly before.

Monday 27 October

Evening: went to Central Hall; heard Rev. Pearse on 'West Country Sketches' portrayed vividly. 'The Methodist Class Meeting', 'the Local Preacher', 'A Sermon' (Cornish); he was very touching in some moments and humorous at others. Perhaps most affecting when

56

speaking of 'love of God.' Said 'We have no rope to fathom the mighty ocean, and asked angels whether there is one in heaven. Answer came back, 'No, there is one on earth.' In astonishment the preacher shouted, 'Where?' Answer came back, 'John 3:16.'[178]

Tuesday 28 October
Went to Free Trade Hall and heard Paderewski[179] (the world famous pianist). He played some pieces which no one else can 'play'. It was marvellous the way in which he played some pieces, the runs seemed to be played with the greatest ease, almost as by machinery; the pathos and excited portions were grand. He seemed to enter into the very soul and interpret the inmost feelings of the great Masters: Chopin, Liszt etc. He had no music before him. In response to the loud applause he played extra pieces. He left off playing one piece and rectified some draught or noise at the doors, which presumably were an annoyance to him. He then started the piece again (so much the better for us.)

Thursday 30 October
With a few exceptions the students went to Didsbury to witness the annual Football Match – 'Prims' v. 'Wesleyans'. It was an intensely exciting match. When goals were scored for us, we raised a mighty shout and vice-versa. Cries of 'Buck up Alec's'[180] and 'Now then Did's' prevailed in keen opposition. For some time the score was 2-2 and we were held in unpleasant suspense. Then we got another and ere long were 5-2. So ended the match, we shouting, waving hats and sticks in proud triumph.

Sunday 2 November
Set myself to get up at 6am; woke about 4, and then 5am; got up at 6 and got ready to go to Bolton[181] (Halliwell)[182] where I was planned. While others were sleeping I had to get ready. Three of us had our breakfast at 7 and at 7.20 I started to catch the train at Victoria Street at 8.25.[183] I had plenty of time and ultimately reached Bolton safely. Had some difficulty in finding way. Called in and had a cup of tea and some bread and butter and reached Halliwell Chapel about 10.30. Not many people in morning and did not have a very good time. I had to perform a not very pleasant duty, at least I did not think so: baptize a child first time. One thing, it did not take me long. In afternoon took class of 20-30 young men and some seemed to have strange ideas about

heaven and punishment. Had a very good service at night; quite enjoyed the service, so did others, judging from their prayers. We had some good singing. Enjoyed myself at my host's. Ultimately found my way back to college 10.20 after a long day.

Monday 3 November
Evening: went to Missionary Meeting[184] at Western Street. Rev. Baldwin[185] spoke. He gave us some interesting information respecting the religious ideas and customs of the Mashukumbwe.[186] Memories of Lynn[187] and Sister Elsie (the late Mrs B.)[188] came very vividly before my mind's eye.

Wednesday 5 November
Gunpowder plot. Had one or two excitable incidents. One or two got a drenching through being too easily enticed out to look up to windows or putting heads out of windows and receiving a shower bath from above.

Thursday 6 November
Sat up late writing home.

Friday 7 November
Retired fairly early but was disturbed by midnight raiders. (Some found their bedrooms locked from within when retiring.) Much noise and continued late (or even early), and bumping[189] at my door. One next morning had to get out of bedroom through fanlight as he had been locked in.

Saturday 8 November
Went up into city.

Sunday 9 November
At Western St.[190] all day. In evening Prof. Peake[191] gave a sermon on The Lord's Supper – 'Do this in remembrance of me.'[192] Third sermon heard on that subject since August. He was very nice and extremely simple.

Monday 10 November
Went to hear Rev. Greenhough MA (Leicester).[193] Enjoyed his sermon on 'He hath given Him a name [which is above] every name: [that at

58

the name of Jesus every knee should] bow.' [194] He appeared a somewhat sarcastic speaker.

Tuesday 11 November
A Great Day: after a short morning's work we hurried off to Central Hall[195] to hear Rev. Hugh Black MA.[196] preach in connection with the anniversary of Central Hall Mission. The Hall was crowded and we were fortunate to obtain a seat. He was not in perfect state of health, and was rather 'low' in some parts, but I liked him exceedingly; he has not a great deal of 'go' or enthusiasm about him, but [is] cool, deliberate, using choice language, reading his sermon but in as nice a manner as I have seen anyone. His text was 'Come thou [with us and we will] do thee good: for the Lord has spoken good concerning] Israel.'[197] Two-fold appeal of Moses, thus of the church. (1) Appeal for your own good, welfare (2) and more pathetic and forcible: for good of the Church. He was rather short; has a young appearance.

In afternoon had to play against Owen's College,[198] and felt miserable, raining nearly all the time and seemed as though I could not play; was glad when it was over. Lost 4-3.

In evening, (after a more bountiful tea than usual, which was very acceptable seeing I had no proper dinner) went to Free Trade Hall, to large meeting in connection with Anniversary Services. We were specially favoured with 2 Boxes, and the Wesleyan Students with 2 others at back of Hall, high above the gallery. It was a sight to see the crowded hall; a very impressive view was thus afforded us, and though right at the back, we could hear very distinctly (almost wonderful). Speakers: Rev. Collier,[199] Rev. Banks,[200] Dr Pierson,[201] Rev. Chadwick (Leeds),[202] Rev. Wiseman (Birmingham).[203] The Dr gave the most intellectual speech, all centering [sic] on 'A perfect Christianity will reproduce itself.' Perhaps Rev. Wiseman took best; he spoke after the Doxology was sung, because of the announcement – £2,516 10s 7d. Rev. Collier asked for £2,500, and 'played to the gallery' as the saying is, but was quite 'Wise' under circumstances. The singing was 'transporting'; did one good.

Wednesday 12 November
We had another treat. A kind gentleman (Mr Longdon) engaged Mr Duxbury,[204] a popular elocutionist to give us an entertainment. We had two very good pianoforte solos and three good vocal solos – one,

'I know that my Redeemer liveth,' by a very accomplished singer. Mr D. gave us first a recital of the Book of Job. This was a very masterly achievement, it was rendered splendidly; he acted the various speakers very well. He also gave us some lighter pieces. 'The bells': this was fine, one imagined they were listening to them, 'the silver,' 'the golden,' the brazen,' 'the iron.' Also a piece he composed consisting of titles of Dickens' books strung together. Also 'little Jack Horner' as Pope, Carlyle, Shakespeare, Dickens, Longfellow and Tennyson would tell it. This was very amusing. Also 'The Last Test Match,' describing a cricket match between two little slum boys and how, after they were promised to be taken to 'a real test match', one got fatally injured and dreamed a dream of playing in a T.T.[205] The former part was very humorous but the latter very sentimental.

Saturday 15 November
Evening: went with party to give a concert at Higher Broughton[206] for the married ladies' effort. Had a good time, but more especially afterwards when we sat down to a bountiful supper. There are very fine premises at H.B.,[207] comparatively new.

Sunday 16 November
Morning: went to Western Street.
Afternoon: addressed the Bible Class at Moss Lane, felt rather nervous, but not as bad as I expected, had fairly nice time. Went to tea and supper with Mr Gosling, very nice folks; had an enjoyable time. Rev. Taylor[208] preached in evening; more of a lecture on Amos than a sermon. They have something like 800 scholars and teachers at Moss Lane.

During the week went into Lewis's.[209] It is a tremendous affair, more like a market than a shop; small stalls dotted here and there. They have men acting as policemen constantly about – so they need.
Some of the men seem to have started to work hard, but Saturday evening they had a break and enjoyed themselves in social intercourse.

Sunday 23 November
Went to Western St. in morning; a very good service. Rev. Neilson preached. He gave out the first hymn, 'O love of God, how strong and true,' and in the congregation were members of a recently bereaved family. I thought, Ah! It is easy for me to sing this glorious hymn, but

60

how difficult for them. I judge they had no heart to sing. God be
merciful and console and cheer such, give them faith and trust to
override apparently insurmountable barriers of grief. Give them the eye
of faith to pierce, penetrate the dark cloud, to see the silver lining of
God's all-wise Providence. I enjoyed the sermon very much. I had read
a similar one on the same text – 1 Kings 8[210] – David's unfulfilled plan:
yet the better for it. In afternoon went to P.S.A.; enjoyed it much.
Mr Neilson gave an address on our relation to our home life, church life
and –.[211]
In evening heard Rev. Softley[212] (Bircham) preach at Withington on
'Daniel's purpose' – temperance sermon. Took tea and supper with
Mr W.;[213] had a grand time.

Monday 24 November
First day of Semenaire.[214]
Work commenced in good earnest.
Recently there has been a slander case which has been tried at the
Assizes.[215] A Member of the City Council made some damaging
references concerning the comedy theatre,[216] so he was summoned by
the proprietor. The case lasted 6 days and many startling stories came
to light concerning the life at the Comedy. The best barristers in the
country were counsels. Marshall Hall[217] appeared for Plaintiff. He made
a wonderful speech. The summing up occupied over 4 hours. The
verdict was given in favour of Defendant. His expenses will be about
£3000[218] and a fund is to be opened for him. What will expenses of
Plaintiff be?

Friday 28 November
Evening: Some gave vent to their feelings and came singing along the
corridor, 11pm or past. One was singing, 'O where is my wandering
girl tonight?' In the upper hermitage there was much noise and the
governor went, but was kept outside some time during which the chief
offender hid under the bed; then the governor went in but little thought
anyone was under the bed. One said he should never forget how
Kinnish[219] 'shot under that bed.'

Saturday 29 November
Saw for the first time a rugby football match,[220] the most comical way
of playing football that could be imagined. To see how they hurl one

another down is not very pleasant; you are all the time expecting to see a bad accident. The scrimmages are also very strange. The players must be exceptionally strong and supple. As a class they looked extremely rough. One or two resembled 'convicts.'

Sunday 30 November
In morning went to Dr Gooderich's[221] and had a good time. He briefly referred to Dr Parker's[222] death. He told a story of an old gentleman who set fire to his rice stacks to attract the villagers, who were busily engaged in preparing for a feast, from the sea coast up the hill. He was successful and immediately, as he had foreseen, the sea came rushing in and overwhelmed the village, it being the result of a slight earthquake.[223] 'Be willing, young people to sacrifice for others' welfare,' was the burden of his exhortation. We had a fine chorus (anthem), 'Yea, though ... walk ... valley.' The sermon was on the 'Paradox of Greatness,' being one of a series. Text: the incident of the mother of Zebedee's children and her request. Matt. 20:26, 'Whosoever ... great ... minister.' He contrasted her greatness with Christ's. (1) In idea (2) In motive (3) In method (4) In result. He appears a fine gentleman, inviting his people to ask young people, strangers to social half-hour after service in evening.
In afternoon went to Cavendish Chapel[224] P.S.A. Rev. Fillingham[225] read lesson and prayed. He is a Church Clergyman who has spoken out against Ritualism. We had a good solo: 'Abide with Me.'
Rev. Leach,[226] the pastor, gave an address on late Dr Parker[227] who was formerly a pastor of the chapel when it possessed several millionaire members. They paid £600 debt of a smaller church to get Dr Parker to come and be their minister; they have today the receipt for that money. Also we heard the letter, very audacious for a young man 27 years old, which he sent to the deacons and it might be summed up in the sentence 'I shall do as I like' i.e. when I come to Cavendish. We have heard several stories concerning him. He was a stone-mason's son. (I am glad I took the opportunity of hearing him in City Temple[228] the previous February.)
In evening I went and preached at Wood St. Mission.[229] They are doing a grand work there.

Tuesday 2 December

Went to Free Trade Hall in evening to a grand Concert.[230] Rode up in electric tram[231] from Alexandra Park for the first time; it is quite an improvement on the horse-tram. Were fortunate to be near the doors, so got in early and had a good seat. There was some splendid talent there, perhaps the most brilliant being Madame Albani,[232] who sang several pieces, including three or four encores. She is a fine person, rather short, and her action amuses one to see her trot on and off the stage; her bows are almost unique, and the way she thrusts forth her hands when finishing a song, especially if ending on a high note. She is a wonderful singer. After she has reached the note that one thinks the highest possible she still reaches a higher. There is also much volume in her music. She sang 'Last Rose of Summer' as an encore. Another talented artiste was Ada Crossley:[233] a fine young lady with a beautiful contralto voice. An exquisite mellow volume of sound poured from her throat. Another, the far-famed bass singer: Mr Santley;[234] he gave us two or three fine songs. Age is creeping upon him. Another vocalist, Mr W. Green,[235] the noted tenor, gave us some of his talent, showing full well that he 'can sing' and sing extremely well.

Another noted performer was Lady Halle,[236] the accomplished violinist; she gave us some 'music', not 'screeching, teeth-edging' noise. She went up to the highest also down to the lowest notes producing fine music. Her instrument appeared to be an exceptionally fine one. This Lady also had a very fine physique. She accompanied Lady Albani once or twice and some perfect harmony resulted. A Mr Cockerill, Harpist, also accompanied in fine style. Miss Adela Verne[237] gave us three or four grand piano solos, rendered in capital style. She reminded me somewhat of Paderewski.[238] The best (if possible) was kept to last. This was a quartet given by the aforesaid vocalists, probably this would be almost the best quartet party it would be possible to produce. It was a masterpiece. How they sang and came in with their own parts was marvellous; it sounded almost like a full chorus. The accompanist, Mr F. J. Watkin deserves mention for the able manner in which he accompanied the songs and quartet.

As we were coming back, the roller slipped the wire and darkness immediately prevailed. A passenger very coolly and promptly inquired whether the conductor 'wanted a match'! This led to much amusement.

Wednesday 3 December
Night. Much excitement prevailed after Supper. One of our men caught the 2nd year man 'tippling beds' and at once gave the alarm. A force of the top corridor men proceeded to the scene of action but the intruders had decamped; from what I heard there was a little scuffling, and presently the governor came, and there was a general scamper, then a stillness. One said it was highly amusing to see them scampering down the steps – you could hardly have thrown them down quicker. The bed-clothes were gone and our men were in a fix. My bed was fortunately untouched – they had just reached the bedroom before mine. After some time the clothes were discovered on 2nd corridor and there was a general march of men ladened with clothes. One remarked he thought he would have an extra blanket and he suddenly discovered the Gov. was watching close by. He was round investigating the affair, but I think unsuccessfully.

Late Friday Evening or early Saturday Morning
Some of them were round on the corridor singing hymns and it sounded so nice that I had to join in with them, though I had almost been to sleep. One night one was singing, 'Where is my wandering girl tonight?'

Saturday 6 December
Afternoon: the 2nd team with one or two 1st team players played Moss Lane F.C. I played and had the success to shoot one goal and assisting in obtaining others. We won 6-0. The ground was hard but no serious accident occurred.

Sunday 7 December
Morning: went to hear Dr Maclaren. Rev. Roberts[239] conducted the (preliminaries) (I don't like the word). The Dr was not quite strong enough.[240] He made a beautiful reference to Rev. H. P. Hughes[241] and Dr Parker's[242] death, saying two brilliant stars had been taken from the firmament. His subject was upon Christ the Light and the smaller lights which receive their illuminating power from Him. Lamps lighted by contact with the uncreated light, soon extinguished. I thought sorrowfully how his lamp which has been shining brilliantly for many years will (if not already) soon flicker and be extinguished. It was a very nice service.

64

In afternoon went to PSA.

Afterwards went to Withington where we again received a warm welcome. Went to Chapel and Rev. Graham[243] preached on 'Create in me ... etc.'[244] Made a neat reference to contrast between 'white-washed' and 'washed white'. In evening had music and conversation and left after spending a very enjoyable time.
'Reference to Adopted (Soeur)'.

Monday 8 December
Worked during the day and in Evening went to Moss Side Baptist Church[245] and heard 'Messiah'. Chorus of about 150 voices special. Principals: Madame A. Radford, Miss A. Paddon,[246] Mr H. Smith, Mr. Pashley. There was a splendid conductor. It was a fine performance. I especially enjoyed the contralto in 'He was despised and rejected of men.' The choruses, 'For unto us a child is born' and 'Hallelujah' were very good. Also Soprano, 'I know that my Redeemer liveth.'

Sunday 14 December
In Morning and Afternoon went to Western St. At P.S.A. had two very good solos.
In Evening went to Dr Gooderich's[247] church. A minister from Bournemouth preached from subject 'Christians in Caesar's household.' He only appeared to have one thought and never got further. It was, 'Therefore you can be a Christian anywhere today.'
This week was exam week and a hard week too. Some up until 2am, others rising about 5am.

Thursday 18 December
Four of us went to hear the 'Messiah.' We were nearly the first at the doors, and when opened hurried up into the Hall and were dismayed to find all seats taken. It was rather uncomfortable, close quarters and standing. The Hall was crowded. I was fortunate in obtaining a good view of the singers. The lady singers were dressed in cream, the gentlemen with low waistcoats. At 7.30 the choir came upon the platform, about 350 voices; also a large and splendid orchestra. Then the soloists and conductor. The principals were Miss Alice Nickolls,[248] Miss Ada Crosseley,[249] Mr Ben Davis [sic][250] and Mr Santley.[251] It was a magnificent performance. The choruses were fine, also the solos, more especially 'All we like sheep', 'Unto us a child', 'Hallelujah',

Miss Nickolls' 'I know that my Redeemer liveth,' Miss Crosseley's 'He was despised,' and 'He shall lead His flock,' and Mr Santley's 'Why do the nations rage.' It was a treat of a lifetime: a pity to miss it: am glad I went.

Friday 19 December
Last exam. What a relief! Had quite enough. Spent afternoon in clearing room and packing up.

Saturday 20 December – the long looked-for day.
Had a nice journey to Ely. Started from Park Station[252] 9.30am. Got to Soham[253] at 5pm.

NOTES TO THE DIARY

[1] The Hull Conference in 1902 decided that the length of the year in residence for students should be increased by five weeks, which may explain why the term started in August.

[2] He was setting out from the family home. His father, Rev. James Davidson, a Primitive Methodist minister, was then stationed at Rockland St. Peter, a village near Stow Bedon, which was to the south-east of Watton, in Norfolk, about 25 miles from King's Lynn. He would have taken a Great Eastern train, running from Thetford to King's Lynn, where he would have needed to change stations, to pick up the Midland & Great Northern Joint Railway (M&GN) for Spalding, for which the trains stopped at South Lynn station. The M&GN Railway was formed in 1893, amalgamating several smaller lines and ran from Great Yarmouth to Peterborough; the trains from South Lynn to Spalding would use a branch going off from Sutton Bridge to Spalding. John Brodbribb, *The Main Lines of East Anglia* (Oxford: Ian Allan Publishing, 2009).

[3] King's Lynn, Norfolk. His father had been stationed at King's Lynn in 1899, where FCD had completed his secondary education at King's Lynn Technical School (see Introduction). He evidently still had friends there.

[4] In March 1882 a new direct line had opened from Spalding to Lincoln, via Sleaford, the Great Northern & Great Eastern Joint Railway. The train would come into Lincoln St. Marks, one of the two stations in Lincoln, the other being Lincoln Central. The cathedral can be seen up the hill from the station. Paul Anderson, *Railways of Lincolnshire* (Oldham: Irwell Press, 1992).

[5] 'Apart from Durham, there is no English cathedral so spectacularly placed as Lincoln. The street by which one approaches it is justly called Steep Hill ... The south view from a distance, e.g. from the railway, is one of singular evenness, the chancel about as long as the nave.' Nikolaus Pevsner and John Harris, *Lincolnshire* (Harmondsworth: Penguin Books, 1964, reprinted 1973), p. 81.

[6] Alec Clifton-Taylor considers Lincoln probably the finest of all English cathedrals. He notes its position, perched on a limestone ridge, visible for miles around, the central tower being, after Boston Stump, the loftiest of the Middle Ages and the most beautiful. The lower parts of the west towers and the central portion of the west front, with friezes of sculpture, are Norman, but essentially it is a thirteenth century building with fourteenth century additions. The cathedral is 482ft. long inside; the crossing tower has a height of 271ft. Alec Clifton-Taylor, *The Cathedrals of England*

(Norwich: Thames and Hudson, 1967, reprinted 1979); Pevsner and Harris, *Lincolnshire*, p. 82.

[7] This may be a reference to the unusual feature in Lincoln Cathedral of two stone doorways with gates from the great transepts into the choir aisles. The carving of leaves in the ornamentation is said to be of exceptional quality. Beyond these is the renowned Angel Choir. Clifton-Taylor, *The Cathedrals of England*, pp. 130-3.

[8] The 'through' (i.e. no change of train and therefore of railway company) train journey to get from Lincoln to London Road Station, Manchester, via a long tunnel suggests that he went on the Great Central Railway, formerly the Manchester, Sheffield and Lincolnshire Railway, via Sheffield and Penistone, which would have taken him through the Peak District and Woodhead Tunnel, which is over three miles long, driven through tough millstone grit. *Railway Clearing House Atlas of England and Wales 1904* (London, 1904; reprinted London: Ian Allan Publishing 2001); W. J. Gordon, *Our Home Railways* (2 vols, London, Frederick Warne & Co., 1910; reprinted London: Bracken Books, 1989) II, p. 141.

[9] The scenery of the Peak district would have been particularly impressive to him, coming, as he did, from the relatively flat East Anglia. The Woodhead tunnel is about 1,000 ft. above sea level, with average gradients of 1:120 for the trains, so not a fast journey. Gordon, *Our Home Railways,* vol. II, p. 148.

[10] Manchester London Road Station was re-named Manchester Piccadilly in 1960. The first station was built on the site in 1842. There was a wide station approach sweeping up to the large square building, which was the main station for travel to London, just over four hours away. The station was shared between the London & North Western Railway Company and the Manchester, Sheffield & Lincolnshire, which became the Great Central Railway. Jonathan Schofield, *Manchester Then and Now* (London: Batsford 2009).

[11] Bradshaw's 1902 timetable shows that a train leaving Lincoln at 3.45pm, travelling via Sheffield and Penistone, is due in at Manchester London Road at 6.20pm. It seems likely that this is the train he caught and it arrived late.

[12] See Introduction for history of the College. The first building was L-shaped, on the corner of Alexandra Road South and Gowan Road. The Gowan Road wing had studies and bedrooms for thirty students on three floors, as described here; the main block on Alexandra Road had domestic quarters in the basement, a lecture room and a small classroom on the

ground floor, and the library and a small classroom above. Built in a style described by architects as 'Early English', the college was an impressive structure of which the Primitive Methodists could feel justly proud. The 1895 Edinburgh Conference gave a quarter of its Jubilee Fund for an extension, which was completed in 1897, which provided a duplication of the study block, a new dining room, lecture room and common room, and the clock tower. Then there were 60 students and 12 extra were taken in 1902. This is the building described here. In 1906, with the aim of providing three-year training, a further extension was added, thanks to the generosity of W. P. Hartley, which included a study block and the chapel. G. E. Milburn, *A School for Prophets* (Manchester: Published by Hartley Victoria College to mark its centenary, 1981).

[13] George Parkin, MA, BD, was principal of the College from 1898 until 1903, when he moved to Oldham. He was President of the Primitive Methodist Conference in 1906. See Introduction p. 14.

[14] Albert Humphries, MA, was appointed tutor at the College in 1902. He was President of the Primitive Methodist Conference in 1926. See Introduction p. 19.

[15] A. S. Peake, who later edited the well-known *Peake's Commentary on the Bible*. See Introduction pp. 15-18.

[16] A vivid impression of A. S. Peake's lectures was given by W. Farndale, a contemporary student: 'In my term Professor Peake dictated his lectures word for word amid a silence only broken by the chiming of the quarters from the clock-tower, or by an occasional question from the floor of the hall. The lecturer's voice would flow in calm, measured fashion, unhurried, unhasty, never metallic or wooden, but vibrant with the feeling suitable to the theme. Now and again would come a pause, pens would drop, and some remark or the telling of a humorous incident would light up the serious topic in hand. Any attempt at ill-timed interruption would be quietly but effectively scotched, but any pertinent query would receive fitting answer, illuminating and satisfying.' 'Impressions of an Early Student', in *Essays in Commemoration* (1956) cited by Wilkinson, *Arthur Samuel Peake,* p. 56 (see Diary n. 83 for biographical information about William Farndale).

[17] See entry on 17 August, Diary n. 40. This seems to be a mock 'Camp meeting' to initiate the new student.

[18] Ernest Edward Fisher (1881-1953), who would have started at Hartley at the same time. He was born at Sedgford, Norfolk into a Methodist home; his father was a Local Preacher and circuit steward. He was stationed in

Andover in 1904 and then served in the following circuits: Great Bardfield, Reading, Louth, Pickering, Barton on Humber, Bishop's Castle, Brompton, Aberdare, Wisbech, Peterborough. He retired in the Peterborough Circuit in 1944. For many years he served on the Connexional Local Preachers' Committee. See Introduction p. 9, for the letter he wrote to my grandmother on hearing of her husband's death. Leary, *PM Ministers*; *Minutes of Conference 1953*.

[19] William Dawson (1878-1970) was born at Cramlington, Northumberland, and after training at the college, in 1904 went into circuit at Motherwell, then served in the following circuits: Bradley Green, Gateshead I, Leicester IV, Chester I, Old Hill, Leicester IV, Leicester Claremont Street, Brownhills, Southwell. He retired to Leicester in 1949. Outside circuit work, he was largely concerned with candidates and students, being on the Hartley College Committee, the Primitive Methodist Students' Examination Committee and the July Committee, and was Candidates' Secretary in the Sunderland and Newcastle upon Tyne and Liverpool Districts. He was gifted intellectually and profited by the training at the college under A. S. Peake, retaining into his nineties an interest in philosophy and theology. When preparing to preach, he never wrote down a word, but he would sit in a chair, or stretch out on the settee, light his pipe, and think through what he wanted to say. After a long ministry and many years of retirement, he died in his ninety-third year. *Minutes of Conference 1971*; Leary, *PM Ministers*.

[20] Edward VII, who was born 9 November 1841, eldest son of Queen Victoria, became king on 22 January 1901, and the coronation, which had to be delayed from the original date in June because the king had appendicitis, took place on 9 August 1902.

[21] Firework displays around the country were part of the coronation celebrations. Although fireworks are believed to have originated in China, they have a long history in Japan, which can be traced back to 1613, when a Chinese merchant with a British envoy from King James I presented fireworks to the shogun Tokugawa Ieyasu and they rapidly gained popularity with the general public in Japan. Japanese fireworks especially feature huge shells or balls, which explode scattering the contents, such as stars or, as described here, animal shapes. www.japan-fireworks.com; www.jnto.go.jp/eng/indepth/cultural/feeljapanesque/fireworks.html, [accessed on 10.11.14].

[22] The impressive Town Hall with its prominent clock-tower was completed in 1877 at a cost of £1,000,000 – the world's most expensive building at the

time. The architect, Alfred Waterhouse, won the design competition less for its appearance than for its practicality, in terms of lighting, ventilation and layout. The style is Victorian Gothic. The clock-tower, at 281 feet high, was until 1962 Manchester's tallest structure. Statues and coats of arms of Manchester worthies (including Agricola who governed Mancunium in 59 CE, Charles Worsley of Platt, a Civil War general and Thomas Potter, the city's first mayor in 1878) are incorporated into the façade. Inside the vaulted entrance are two grand staircases. The Great Hall features a series of twelve murals by the Pre-Raphaelite artist Ford Maddox Brown, a Manchester resident, depicting themes from the city's history. The whole building, which is now Grade I listed, is a monument to Manchester's Victorian wealth and influence. John H. G. Archer, 'A Classic of its Age', in John H. G. Archer (ed.), *Art and Architecture in Victorian Manchester*, p. 127; Stuart Hylton, *A History of Manchester*, pp. 192-3; Cecil Steward, *The Stones of Manchester*. See also Introduction p. 24.

23 The Royal Exchange in Manchester was a striking building with an imposing classical portico, designed by a local practice, Mills and Murgatroyd. In the early twentieth century, Manchester, through the private Royal Exchange Company, controlled up to 80 per cent of the world's cotton trade, and the main trading room in this building was said to be the largest commercial room anywhere; international traders, known as merchants, would gather on Tuesdays and Fridays, which were exchange days. In 1902 the number of merchants in Manchester was 804, rising to 1,034 in 1922. The Exchange closed in 1968 and is now home to the Royal Exchange Theatre. Douglas A. Farnie, 'The role of merchants as prime movers in the expansion of the cotton industry 1760-1990,' in Douglas A. Farnie and David J. Jeremy (eds), *The Fibre that Changed the World* (Oxford: Oxford University Press, 2004), pp. 30-31; Schofield, *Manchester Then and Now*, p. 19.

24 Electric cars were a novelty at the turn of the century. Although inventors had been experimenting with electrically powered vehicles for some years, the 'Flocken Elektrowagen' of 1888 by the German inventor Andreas Flocken is regarded as the first real electric car in the world. Only after 1920 did the development of petrol-fuelled cars come to dominate the market. *Encyclopedia Britannica.*

25 A new phenomenon, described in unfamiliar language. Today we would say 'lamp bulbs' or 'light bulbs'.

26 This means that it had been arranged for him to take services on the circuit plan. To take services on some Sundays would be part of the training.

[27] Brookbottom is a small hamlet above the Goyt valley, to the south-east of Manchester, between New Mills in Derbyshire and Marple in Cheshire, where a PM minister was stationed (in the Manchester District). The chapel was built in 1874, and the vestry added in 1884. Opposite is a large building, once the chapel schoolroom, which has now been converted into houses. The village is in an isolated spot today, on the edge of the Peak District, but there would have been a number of mills in the valley then. The village population found employment at the local calico printworks in the valley, Strines Print Works, which in 1902 employed up to 600 people. By the early 1890s, Britain's calico industry printed 1,500 to 2,000 million yards per annum, of which 900 to 1,000 million yards were for export. David J. Jeremy, 'Working the Business as One: Cultural and Organisational Aspects of the Calico Printers' Association Merger of 1899', in John F. Wilson (ed.), *King Cotton: A Tribute to Douglas A. Farnie* (Lancaster: Crucible Books, 2009).

[28] Whitworth Park, named after Sir Joseph Whitworth, the man who discovered the method of producing a truly plane surface, was a 20 acre piece of land acquired in 1887 and laid out as a park, within which an institute of art and industry was to be established. In 1913 a bronze statue of Edward VII by J. Cassidy was unveiled in its grounds. See Hartwell, *Manchester,* p. 312.

[29] Alexander Maclaren (1826-1910) was a well-known Baptist minister and scholar, born in Glasgow, into a Scottish Baptist family. Following a period of ministry in Southampton, in 1858 he accepted an invitation to the pastorate at Union Chapel, Manchester, where he remained for 45 years until his retirement in 1903. Here he became widely known as a fine preacher and expositor of Scripture. After he had been there eleven years, a new 1,500-seat auditorium was built and every seat was filled, morning and evening. Twice President of the Baptist Union, he presided at the Baptist World Congress in London in 1905. Through all this he remained a shy, diffident man, who did not find the pastoral side of ministry easy. Although the Union Chapel in Oxford Road is no longer standing, his high pulpit survives as a memorial to him within the Union Chapel, Fallowfield. Over 400 of his sermons have been published in book form; after his retirement in 1903, he rarely preached, but he undertook a 31-volume pastoral commentary, *Expositions of Holy Scripture.* J. Y. H. Briggs, in *BDE*, pp. 397-9.

[30] Union Chapel, Oxford Road. When Alexander Maclaren came to be pastor, the congregation was in a smaller building further along Oxford Road, which was later owned by the United Free Methodists. They moved to their new building in 1869.

[31] Owens College, named after John Owens, a Manchester textile merchant who left a large bequest for the purpose, was founded in 1851 and later became the University of Manchester (see Introduction p. 25). The Museum which was housed there had originally been a collection of the Manchester manufacturer John Leigh Philips (1761-1814), which after his death was housed, with further donations, in Peter Street. In 1850 it absorbed the collection of the Manchester Geological Society. By the 1860s the building was full and its administration was transferred in 1867 to Owens College. In 1888 the museum was moved to a new building in Oxford Street designed by Alfred Waterhouse, architect of the Natural History Museum in London. The museum is now known as Manchester Museum. Hartwell, *Manchester*, p. 111.

[32] See Introduction p. 23 on the city of Manchester and the pollution caused by industry.

[33] Ernest Fisher, a student in the same year and his closest friend (see Diary n. 18).

[34] The Whitworth Art Gallery, opened in 1890, was designed by J. W. Beaumont. It is a large, impressive building, with a semi-circular colonnade of granite in the Renaissance style, oriel windows that are in the Elizabethan style, buttresses that are Henry VIII and a 'lantern' that is Queen Anne. It was a monument to Sir Joseph Whitworth (see Diary n. 28 on Whitworth Park). In time the gallery became internationally renowned for its British water colours and unique range of textiles. See Francis W. Hawcroft, 'The Whitworth Art Gallery', in Archer (ed.), *Art and Architecture in Victorian Manchester*, pp. 208-29; Steward, *The Stones of Manchester*.

[35] Important and necessary advice in the social, political and cultural context of the Empire. Missionary work, facilitated by colonial expansion, had seen huge progress in the nineteenth century in many areas of the world where other religions, such as Islam, Buddhism and Hinduism had been traditionally practised for centuries. James Mott, the American who chaired the first World Missionary Conference in Edinburgh, had inspired a generation in the 1880s and 90s with the slogan, 'The Evangelisation of the World in this Generation,' and in 1910 this did not seem an impossible dream. However, different voices were beginning to be heard. In 1893, Swami Vivekananda spoke at the Parliament of Religions held in that year in Chicago, pleading for mutual recognition of the spirituality of East and West; there should be fellowship in sympathy but no attempt at proselytism. 'People should be treated with dignity,' he said. 'They are not "anonymous Christians"; holiness, purity and chastity are not the exclusive

possessions of any church in the world and every system has produced men and women of the most exalted character.' Some missionaries were not unsympathetic to this view; scholarship was revealing the spiritual treasures of ancient religions and a more liberal theology took a rather different view of the uniqueness of Christianity from that which had been current in earlier days. Alan P. F. Sell, *Confessing and Commending the Faith* (Cardiff: University of Wales Press, 2002), pp. 361ff; Stephen Neill, *Christian Missions* (Harmondsworth: Penguin Books, 1964), pp. 358-9.

[36] The kind of liberal theology, that regarded all religions as spokes of a wheel, all leading to the hub, could be open to the criticism that, while it was good to build bridges, aspects that were mutually contradictory could in the process be overlooked. Sell, *Confessing and Commending the Faith*, pp. 361ff.

[37] Mr Wightman and Mr Hooson were fellow students. Arthur Wightman went into circuit in Liverpool in 1904 and moved to Oldham in 1908, after which there is no further information. Leary, *Primitive Methodist Ministers*.

[38] George Stewart Hooson (1881-1961) was born at Wootton Bassett in Wiltshire and educated at Bourne College, Quinton. He left Hartley in 1903 to go to Walkden and then served in the following circuits: Stoke Newington, Hornsea, Doncaster I, Wigan, Pudsey, Hartlepool W., Swindon II, Scunthorpe, Epworth West, Barnsley W., Pudsey. Having received a sound education in elocution early in life, together with a keen sense of drama and humour, he became well-known for his literary recitals, which brought much gain, both material and spiritual, to his circuits in the North. He retired in 1947, but continued to preach in Brighouse, Ticehurst and Tunstall. *Minutes of Conference 1961*; Leary, *Primitive Methodist Ministers*.

[39] The City Art Gallery in Moseley Street was designed in 1824-5 by Charles Barry (who went on to design the Palace of Westminster) for the Manchester Institution for the Promotion of Science, Literature and the Arts, and acquired for the city in 1882, along with their extensive collections, and opened to the general public. It was endowed with £4,000 per annum to spend on new works. The building marks the climax of Greek revival architecture in the city. Hartwell, *Manchester*, pp. 89-91; Schofield, *Manchester Then and Now*, p. 61.

[40] Camp Meetings are large evangelistic meetings in the open air, and were a feature of North American Methodist revivalism. Introduced to England by Lorenzo Dow, they were a cause of the split between Primitive and Wesleyan Methodists. The first official 'Camp Meeting', organized by Hugh Bourne, was held at Mow Cop in 1807. Official opposition, however,

to revivalism was hardening. The Methodist Conference of 1807 condemned 'Camp Meetings' as being likely to foster indiscipline and uncontrolled initiatives among the lay membership. However, Hugh Bourne continued to advocate them and was expelled from Wesleyan Methodism in 1808. As the Primitive Methodist movement gathered strength, 'Camp Meetings' were a characteristic feature. Milburn, *Primitive Methodism*, pp. 6, 9-12.

[41] Ernest Edward Fisher (see Diary n. 18).

[42] Mr Wright.

[43] The collegiate church of St. Mary, St. Denys and St. George became a cathedral in 1847, at a time when the population of Manchester, which was already about 200,000, was expanding rapidly. The building had become a very wide parish church in the fifteenth century, with double aisles added to the nave, and to the north the buildings for the new college of priests, which was set up in 1421. In the seventeenth century these buildings were turned into a new hospital and school by Humphrey Chetham. The large west tower (130 feet high) was rebuilt in 1864 and major restoration work done in 1882. A new porch was added in 1897, but lack of space prevented any further expansion to the east, in contrast to many other newly created northern cathedrals, so the overall impression is still one of a large parish church. A notable feature inside is the fine late medieval and early Tudor woodwork, including beautifully carved choir-stalls, screen and roof. Tim Tatton-Brown and John Crook, *The English Cathedral* (London: New Holland, 2002).

[44] Exchange Station is across the road from the cathedral. It was opened in 1884 by the London and North Western Rail Company after a plan to share the nearby Victoria station fell through. As a result one of the platforms on the Leeds-Liverpool line was the longest in the world at 730 yards. Jonathan Schofield, *Manchester Then and Now*.

[45] Lewis' department stores originated from Liverpool (a different firm from John Lewis). David Lewis arrived in Liverpool in 1839, son of a capable Jewish merchant in London. After working for a tailoring firm, in 1856, he opened his first shop in Ranelagh Street, Liverpool, and took advantage of the growing population to expand the business and create a new-style department store in Bold Street, involving his nephews in the family-run business. On the basis of this success, he opened new stores in Manchester, Birmingham and Sheffield. Although the venture in Sheffield failed eventually, in Manchester their first shop in Market Street, which opened on 13 January 1880 was an instant success and over the years various

extensions were built. It was the first store to bring large-scale shopping to Manchester, combining aggressive advertising, bulk-buying and low prices, aimed at the upper-working and lower middle-classes. It steadily expanded its range of goods and combined retailing with manufacture, so that by the 1880s, as well as 400 shop assistants, there were 300 tailors and 200-300 people making boots operating from the store. They aimed to make the store itself an exciting place to visit, so that in 1897 it was one of the first venues in Manchester to show the new 'Cinematographe' developed by the Lumière brothers and once even flooded their basement to offer Venetian gondola rides. See Hylton, *A History of Manchester*, p. 223; Asa Briggs, *Friends of the People: The Centenary History of Lewis's* (London: B. T. Batsford, 1956), pp. 27-68.

[46]   Great Western Street seems to have been the nearest Primitive Methodist Church to the college and the one FCD attends most frequently. It was situated in Moss Side, but no longer exists today.

[47]   Daniel Neilson (1850-1904) was appointed to the Manchester VI circuit in 1898. See Introduction pp. 19-20.

[48]   John Kinnish (1877-1949) was born at Malew on the Isle of Man. He was accepted for the ministry and, after training at Hartley, went into circuit in 1903 and served in ten circuits: Newtown, Manchester V, Newbury, Stoke-on-Trent, Clay Cross, Ashton-under-Lyne, Wolverhampton II, Coventry I, Hasbury and Halesowen, and Kidderminster. He married Florence Annie Dinning and they had one son. His ministry was marked by great devotion and ability; his sermons were said to be fresh and rich in thought, giving evidence of his well-trained mind and Christian experience. He retired in 1942, due to ill-health, to Wolverhampton, after thirty-nine years in circuit, and died in 1949. *Minutes of Conference 1949*; Leary, *Primitive Methodist Ministers*.

[49]   David Cooke (1878-1957) was accepted for the ministry from the Gateshead circuit. He left the college in 1904 to go into circuit in Leicester and after that served in the following circuits: Middlesbrough, N. Shields, Birmingham V, Birkenhead I, St. Anne's on Sea, Leeds Armley. A breakdown in health caused his retirement to St. Anne's in 1939. During his ministry he served on District Committees of Candidates and Probationers, and for ten years was on the PM Candidates Committee, being the Connexional Secretary for five years. See also mention in Diary on 24 September. Leary, *Primitive Methodist Ministers*; *Minutes of Conference 1958*.

[50]   James Palmer (1877-1967) was born in Durham. His family moved to Stanley, Co. Durham, where he started work in the coal mine at the age of twelve. Converted at a service at the little wayside chapel at Oxhill, he

educated himself to the standard required to candidate for the ministry. After training at Hartley, he left for the Normanton Circuit in 1904. He then served in the following circuits: Shipley, Burnopfield, Jarrow, Allendale, Newcastle III, Durham and Spennymoor, retiring to Durham in 1943. His ministry was spent in the North East, where he was greatly loved and accepted by shipyard workers, farmers and miners alike, because of his deep human understanding. While preaching in retirement, he suddenly went blind during a service, but continued to the end, reciting lessons and preaching the sermon from memory. His disability did not daunt him; he continued visiting the local hospital and remained active until a few days before his death in his ninetieth year. *Who's Who in Methodism, 1933; Minutes of Conference 1967.*

[51] Abraham Hill (1880-1952) was born in Wigan. After training at Hartley, he served in twelve circuits, mostly in East Anglia: Chelmsford, Ipswich and Hadleigh, Sheringham and Holt, Acle, Bury St. Edmunds, Colchester, Haslingden, Wangford, Acle again, Martham, Aylsham and Fakenham, before retiring to Martham in 1949. During his twelve years at Acle, a revival broke out in Freethorpe, one of the villages, when several young men and women were brought into the church. He also had an outstanding ministry at Aylsham, where he stayed nine years. *Who's Who in Methodism, 1933; Minutes of Conference 1953.*

[52] Presumably Kinnish (see Diary n. 48).

[53] Piccolo?

[54] By the end of the nineteenth century, the 'Pleasant Sunday Afternoons' movement was a recognised force in Nonconformity and centred on talks, normally by the minister or a guest speaker, and aimed at men only. There was a concentration on current affairs, normally seen from a liberal viewpoint. Their motto was 'Brief, Bright and Brotherly'. Musical items were part of the programme and such meetings continued until the mid-twentieth century in some chapels. See James Munson, *The Nonconformists: In Search of a Lost Culture* (London: SPCK, 1991), p. 63.

[55] Alexandra Park, nearly opposite the college.

[56] Baptist Chapel in Oxford Road (see Diary n. 30 on 11 August).

[57] John Edward Roberts (1866-1929) was junior pastor, or co-pastor, of Union Chapel. He was born at Bootle, but he spent his childhood in London, where his father Robert Henry Roberts, was minister at Ladbroke Grove, President of the Baptist Union in 1892, and Principal of Regent's Park College in 1893. John matriculated at London University when he was sixteen, and a year later entered Regent's Park College. In 1890 he left

to go to assist Alexander Maclaren at Union Chapel, but he continued his academic work and in 1895 took the BD degree at St. Andrew's University. In 1920 the same university made him Doctor of Divinity. He was elected successor to Maclaren upon his resignation in 1903 and served there for fifteen years. In 1918 he became minister at Adelaide Place in Glasgow. He died unexpectedly on 25 January 1929. (Information supplied by Emily Burgoyne, Angus Library, Regent's Park College, Oxford).

[58]   See Diary n. 39, on 16 August.

[59]   The painting referred to is probably '*The Shadow of Death*', painted by William Holman Hunt (1827-1910) in the early 1870s, showing the young Jesus working in his earthly father's carpentry shop, casting a shadow that seems to predict the crucifixion. In 1882 the Manchester Corporation Act put into effect the proposal that the Corporation should receive the transfer of the collection and premises of the Royal Manchester Institution in Mosley Street and provide the Art Gallery Committee with £2,000 p.a. for purchases for the next 20 years. Among the acquisitions in 1884 was this painting by Holman Hunt. It is now in Manchester Art Gallery. Stuart Macdonald, 'The Royal Manchester Institution' in Archer (ed.) *Art and Architecture in Victorian Manchester* pp. 43-5; Manchester Art Gallery website: www.manchestergalleries.org.

[60]   *Work* is a painting by Ford Madox Brown (1821-93), completed in 1865, depicting, in the centre, navvies working, observed by him in Hampstead in 1852, with children and passers-by around them. The moral value of work was much discussed in the middle of the nineteenth century, so these workers are surrounded by those who do not need to work or are deprived of meaningful work. In contrast, on the right, Thomas Carlyle, author of *Past and Present,* on the nobility of labour, converses with F. D. Maurice, founder of the first college for working men. Their thinking produces purposeful work and happiness in others. This is also in the Manchester Art Gallery, acquired before 1900. Elizabeth Conran, 'Art Collections', in Archer (ed.), *Art and Architecture in Manchester*, p. 79; www.manchestergalleries.org.

[61]   See Diary n. 45, on 18 August.

[62]   William Paulden began trading in Stretford Road in the 1860s and the family firm continued to do business in the area until 1957, when the large store built in 1879 on Cavendish Street was totally destroyed in a fire. Paulden was an innovator, and his store was the first to introduce electric lighting, lifts, escalators, plate glass windows and motorized vehicles. He had a moving picture show in the window, presumably advertising goods and services, and the store was reputed to have its own three-piece band. He was even said to

78

be the first to bring Danish pastries to England. Website: manchesterhistory.net/manchester/gone/pauldens.html [accessed 10.11.14].

[63] Blackburn is in Lancashire, about 21 miles north-west of Manchester. It has a long tradition of textile manufacture, and its most rapid growth occurred as a result of the industrialisation and expansion of the textile industry in the nineteenth century. Between the mid-eighteenth century and the early twentieth century the population increased from less than 5,000 to over 130,000. The prosperity was short-lived though. In 1904 a slump hit the cotton industry and a further decline in 1908 saw 43 mills stop production. The closure of mills and subsequent unemployment continued through the first half of the twentieth century. Derek Beattie, *Blackburn: A History* (Lancaster: Carnegie Publishing, 2007).

[64] He would use the Manchester-based Lancashire and Yorkshire Railway, which ran trains from Manchester to Blackpool. The Lancashire and Yorkshire Railway was for many years notorious for trains that were dirty, slow and unpunctual, but this had begun to change after 1883, with new management. In 1886, J. A. F. Aspinall, as locomotive superintendent, began a major programme of producing modern steam locomotives and in 1888-9 new lines bypassed Bolton and Wigan, allowing many services to be accelerated. Early in the twentieth century, the best expresses took just 65 minutes for the run from Manchester to Blackpool. Railway Clearing House, *Atlas of England and Wales,* 1904; David Wragg, *A Historical Dictionary of the Railways in the British Isles* (Barnsley: Wharncliffe Books, 2009).

[65] Granville Road in Blackburn contains fine-looking Victorian terraced houses with large bay windows.

[66] The 1901 census shows that Joseph Hindle, then aged 36, had a chemist's shop; his wife Sarah, 36, was a milliner and they had two children, Gertrude, 15, and James, 11. So the Miss Hindle, who prepared supper, would be Gertrude, aged 16 in 1902.

[67] Oxford Street Chapel, Higher Audley, was opened in 1873 on the site of the former Maudley Street School and Chapel (which had been opened in 1867, but within three years had become overcrowded). The cornerstone of the new, more spacious, chapel was laid by John Hindle, presumably from the same family as his host. The interior of the chapel, which seated 600, measured 60ft x 42ft. and was galleried around. The former chapel continued to be used as a school building, and a further school building was attached to the east end of the chapel. William Alexander Abram, *Parish of Blackburn, County of Lancaster: A History of Blackburn, Town and Parish* (Blackburn: J. G. & J. Toulmin, 1877), p. 47.

79

[68] King's Lynn, where his father would have been minister.

[69] This may be a reference to the Montague Street Chapel and School, since Prince's Street runs along the back of Montague Street. The PM Chapel in Montague Street opened in 1837, schoolrooms were attached in 1871, and then larger schoolrooms were built contiguous with the chapel in 1875. There was seating for 500. Abram, *Parish of Blackburn*, p. 47.

[70] From this information it is not possible to identify definitely the Bolton family, as there are many people of that name in Blackburn. The most likely identification from the 1901 census is James Bolton, aged 67, a former builder and his wife Margaret, aged 60, who lived at 38 Regent Street with two daughters, one aged 29 and another 26, a nurse at the hospital, as well as a son. Regent Street would be within walking distance of Prince's Street. Another possibility is John Bolton, a shopkeeper, who, in 1901, lived with his wife Alice, his daughter Ethel, who was 18, and another daughter Annie, 8, at 395 Whalley New Street (1901 census).

[71] It is not easy to read this word, which is followed by (10/-).

[72] 'Christian Endeavour' was a non-denominational movement begun in America in 1881 Francis E. Clarke, a Congregational minister. It provided fellowship and training for young people and flourished in England in Nonconformist churches, particularly Primitive Methodist ones, where it paralleled the Wesley Guild in the Wesleyan connexion. Vickers, in *Dictionary of Methodism*, p. 64.

[73] Charles Thomas Bishell (1879-1958) was born at Lincoln and educated in Hull; he was a teacher for a few years before being accepted for the ministry and training at Hartley. In 1903 he went into circuit at Stalybridge, and was then stationed as follows: Bollington, Southfield, Leeds VI, Bridlington, Chaplain to H.M. Middle East Forces (1917-19), Bridlington, Scarborough, Church Gresley, Leeds (Cardigan) and Leeds (Richmond). He married Beatrice J. Fell and they had one son (who was lost on active service with the RAF in the Second World War, a severe blow) and one daughter. He retired to Scarborough in 1947, where he served as chaplain to Scarborough Hospital until a short time before his death. *Minutes of Conference 1958*; Leary, *Primitive Methodist Ministers*.

[74] The Smithfield Market, which dominated the area bounded by Shude Hill, Swan Street, High Street, Oak Street and Thomas Street had been there since the late eighteenth century as an open-air market, but in 1853 was covered by an iron and glass roof. By 1897 it covered 4½ acres and, as a wholesale and retail market, provided fresh fruit and vegetables, meat and

fish for the whole region. The Smithy Door Market, later known as Victoria Market, consisted of rows of stalls along either side of Victoria Street, where fruit and vegetables were sold. Hylton, *History of Manchester*, p. 167; Schofield, *Manchester Then and Now*, pp. 14-15.

[75] The Technical School grew out of the Mechanics Institute, which had opened in 1856 with a new building in what is now Princess Street. By the 1870s it was struggling with few enrolments but a bootmaker, J. H. Reynolds, rescued it; appointed as its secretary in 1879, he made it part of a growing national movement for technical education, linking it with the new City and Guilds Examination and soliciting industrial support. It was taken over by the Council in 1892, and a fine new building, of German inspiration, by Spalding & Cross was opened in 1902. Its aim was to teach science for industrial application, while Owens College would teach the professional men. There was an agreement to that effect in 1896, but as money and equipment poured into the new 'Tech', the boundaries were blurred. In later years it became the main building for UMIST, which in 2004 became part of the University of Manchester. Hartwell, *Manchester,* p. 122; Schofield, *Manchester Then and Now*, pp. 54-5; University of Manchester website [accessed 26.02.15]: www.manchester.ac.uk/discover/history-heritage/history/umist.

[76] The warehouses were a distinctive architectural feature of Manchester (see Introduction p. 24).

[77] The Manchester Police Courts, now called the Minshull Street Crown Court, was a complex of buildings on Minshull Street, designed 1867-73 by Thomas Worthington, who submitted his designs for the Town Hall competition in the same year. The style is European Gothic, with a tall corner tower and a chimney stack styled as a campanile. The Courts were constructed in red brick with sandstone dressings and steeply pitched slate roofs. Fierce carved beasts, created by Earp and Hobbs, meet the eye at the entrances. Hartwell, *Manchester*, pp. 172-3.

[78] This is the friend from Withington PM chapel, who offered him hospitality soon after he arrived. See 17 August and 7 September.

[79] This is either a gift from the chapel congregation or a family present. The 1901 census shows his mother, as head of the household, and three brothers living at Rose Cottage, Fincham. This was the address in the PM Minutes for his father, James Davidson, for the years 1900 and 1901, but it is not clear where he was at the time of the 1901 census. By 1902 he had moved to Rockland, but his wife may still have been in the house in Fincham, which was possibly owned by a relative, as the neighbouring land was

81

farmed by someone of the name Collen (her maiden name). The family had had two moves in three years, and probably she would have wanted some stability for the family and for the sake of the children's education. By the 1911 census they were together at Swaffham (see Introduction n. 6).

[80] Congregational Chapel, just north of the junction of Moss Lane with Chorlton Road and Withington Road, on Ayres Road and South Croston Street. The chapel was founded in 1861. At the end of the nineteenth century it had a large Sunday School Hall on the other side of South Croston Street. In 1972, with the union between the Congregational and English Presbyterian Churches, it became a United Reformed Church, but it is now closed. Andrew Simpson: chorltonhistory.blogspot.co.uk [accessed 07.11.14].

[81] Albert Goodrich (1840-1919) was a Congregational Minister in Manchester. He was born in Kingsland, London, and as a young man assisted in the family upholstery business. Although brought up in the Episcopalian Church, he became a Congregationalist, attending Old Tabernacle. At 21, he felt the call and went for training to the Hackney Theological College, then served in Braintree, Essex (1865-76) and at Elgin Place, Glasgow (1876-86), where he became well-known in the city and university, which in 1884 honoured him with the DD degree. In 1886 he became Chair of the Congregational Union in Scotland, then came to the Chorlton Road Chapel in Manchester in 1890, where he stayed until he retired to Colwyn Bay in 1912. He was Chairman of the Congregational Union of England and Wales in 1904. Although Nonconformists had been against aggressive imperial expansion, towards the end of the nineteenth century this began to change, and in 1898, Goodrich, when addressing the Congregational assembly, instead of giving his prepared speech regarding international arbitration in the Sudan crisis, called upon France to retire, amid cheers. *Congregational Yearbook 1920*; Bebbington, *The Nonconformist Conscience*, p. 121.

[82] Luke 22:19.

[83] William Farndale DD, (1881-1966) was born at York and became a student at Hartley in 1902. He was a very able student who gained top marks in examinations. He served in the following circuits: Forest Hill, Oldham II, Chester-le-Street, Birkenhead II, Grimsby II, and then from 1933 he was Lincoln District Missionary and Chairman of the Lincoln and Grimsby District. He was President of Conference in 1947 and initiated the Call of the Countryside and a 'Back to the Soil' campaign. His administrative gifts were matched by his love for rural Methodism and the farming community.

During his presidency he attended the Methodist Ecumenical Conference in Massachusetts and went as visiting preacher to the United Church of Canada. In 1950-1 he was Moderator of the Free Church Council. On his retirement he became a tutor at Cliff College, where his biblical scholarship assisted many students. *Minutes of Conference 1966*; Leary, *Primitive Methodist Ministers*.

[84] Frederick Brotherton Meyer (1847-1929) was a well-known Baptist minister, scholar and evangelical preacher. Born in Clapham, London, he was the son of a businessman, and educated at Brighton College. His family attended Bloomsbury Chapel, an outward-looking Baptist Church, and Meyer was baptised as a believer at New Park Road Chapel, Brixton in 1864. He studied at Regent's Park College, Oxford from 1866 and graduated from the University of London in 1869. He then pastored churches in Liverpool and York, where he met Dwight Moody and the two became life-long friends. Under Moody's influence, he felt freed from traditional thinking about ministry and came to believe that evangelism should be his own priority. In 1874 he moved to Victoria Road Baptist Church in Leicester, but his commitment to reaching industrial workers outside the life of the church was not shared by most of the congregation and he resigned after four years, intending to leave the city, but was persuaded by some members to stay and form a new church, Melbourne Hall, on the city outskirts. The congregation quickly grew to 1,500, and he did notable work with prisoners, helping 4,500 by the time he left in 1888, employing them on discharge in two businesses he had established, a firewood business and a window-cleaning service. His next pastorate was Regent's Park Chapel in London, followed by Christ Church, Lambeth, where he stayed fifteen years, building up the congregation from 100 to 2,000. He was a strong opponent of the Education Bill (see Introduction p. 25). He began travelling on evangelistic tours, which included South Africa, Asia and North America; as part of the Higher Life Movement he was a frequent speaker at the Keswick Convention, and at the same time a crusader against immorality, especially drunkenness and prostitution. He was President of the Baptist Union in 1906-7. In 1910 he became honorary secretary of the National Free Church Council and to some he seemed to personify the 'Nonconformist Conscience'. Peace issues were important to him and, though not a pacifist, during the First World War relayed to Asquith concerns about the ill-treatment of conscientious objectors. In 1917 he launched the Advent Testimony and Preparation Movement, predicting the Second Coming in 1918. He wrote over seventy books, including *The Way into the Holiest, Expositions into the Epistle to the Hebrews, The Secret of Guidance* and *Christian Living*. I. M. Randall in *BDE*, pp. 428-30.

[85] This could be Public Service workers, or Prison Service workers, or have another significance.

[86] Later in life he gives as his interests music and games. *Who's Who in Methodism in 1933.*

[87] This is probably due to his illness, which necessitated an operation (see Introduction p. 18).

[88] In 1902, the college accounts show that the college employed a cook, a kitchen maid, two college maids, two laundry maids, a housemaid, a gardener and a boy (see Introduction p. 21).

[89] Col. 3:3.

[90] See Diary n. 54.

[91] Daniel Neilson (see Introduction pp. 19-20).

[92] E. E. Fisher, another first-year student, probably his closest friend (see Diary n. 18).

[93] Ridgway Street is in Miles Platting, an area east of the city centre; it is situated between the Rochdale and Ashton Canals, running between Butler Street and Varley Street. This area contained many large mills, and by the 1870s also had chemical works, a timber yard, gas works and a tannery. The volume of industry led to the construction of densely packed back-to-back terraced houses to provide homes for the workers. The area was also dominated by the Lancashire & Yorkshire Railway, with many sidings. In such an area of poverty and deprivation, the mission would provide social, material and spiritual support. Website [accessed 26.02.15]: www.lan-opc.org.uk/Manchester/Miles-Platting/index.html.

[94] See Diary n. 39 on 16 August.

[95] George Emmett (1873-1959), who, after training at Hartley, went to the Manchester IX circuit in 1901. His subsequent circuits were Newcastle III, Stalybridge, Northwich, Stoke & Longton, Oldham III, Walkden, Chorley, and Wigan, and he retired to Harrogate in 1938, where he was happy to continue preaching. He was widely-read and his sense of humour enlivened his conversations and sermons. He died quite suddenly in his eighty-sixth year. *Minutes of Conference 1960*; Leary, *Primitive Methodist Ministers.*

[96] James Bernard of Rusholme, Manchester. The actor Robert Donat, who was born in Withington, was a pupil of the 'well-known Manchester elocutionist, James Bernard, under whom he received stage training and elocution lessons, which helped him to shed both his stutter and his broad

Lancashire accent'. Papers of Robert Donat, John Rylands University Library (identification: GB133FRD).

[97] Belle Vue is still a sports and leisure centre east of Manchester city centre, with its own station. In 1902 it was a major attraction in Manchester. John Jennison (b. 1793) took on the lease in 1836 of the area of a site between Stockport Road and Hyde Road with a view to creating a leisure area similar to his venture in his native Nottinghamshire. Although the earlier years landed him in debt, with the help of the railway running cheap trains to the station at Longsight, he was able to develop the site to include lakes, where spectacular fireworks displays were held and historic events were acted out with scenery and pyrotechnic effects, a growing zoological collection and a natural history museum. Early in the twentieth century, attractions included a circus ring and fairground, a cinematograph and a roller-skating rink. Stuart Hylton, *A History of Manchester*, pp. 134-6.

[98] Stanley King Chesworth (1878-1961) was born at Longsight, Manchester of Anglican parents. He became a Primitive Methodist in his teens, and following a call to preach, became a Hired Local Preacher in the Leeds (Belle Vue) PM Circuit. He entered the Manchester College in 1902, the same time as FCD, and left in 1904 to go to the Harrow and Northwood Mission, then served in Bedale, Dalton and Millom, Motherwell, Brandon, Buckley, Laxey, Fincham, Brampton, Colne, Manchester IV, Bloxwich Pinfold, Bolton Moor Lane, and Littleborough. Advised in 1937, after serious illness, never to preach again, he continued with indomitable courage and zeal for eleven more years in the full work and five years as an active supernumerary at Failsworth, before retiring to Bloxwich in 1953, where he continued to preach as long as strength allowed. He was a keen temperance reformer and brought salvation to some as he worked among alcoholics in Manchester's Piccadilly. He died in May 1961 at the age of 82. *Minutes of Conference 1961*; Leary, *Primitive Methodist Ministers*.

[99] Chorlton-cum-Hardy PM Church in High Lane was registered for worship between 1897 and 1972. It is not clear if this is the same church, but if it is, it closed in 1960 and was destroyed by arson in 1967. Manchester Archives, accession numbers: 1997/50 and 1998/1a; website; discover.nationalarchives.gov.uk [accessed 26.02.15].

[100] Thomas Mitchell, DD, (1844-1915) was President of the Primitive Methodist Conference in 1902. He was born at Low Moor, near Bradford, but soon moved to Barnsley. After work in the Sunday School and as a Local Preacher, he was recommended for the ministry and trained for a year at Elmfield College, York. He served in the following circuits: Saffron Walden,

Barnsley, Bradford II, Halifax, Bingley, Burnley, Hull I, Hull V, Hull II, 1895 Book Steward, Leeds II, 1901 Secretary of CEF, Southport. He became Financial Secretary to the Missionary Society, Secretary of Conference, and administered various church funds. An able and effective preacher, he was also a wise administrator and helpful pastor. He was President of the National Free Church Council in 1912. *Primitive Methodist Minutes 1915.*

[101] Colloquial for 'we travelled by train'. This use of the intransitive verb 'train', to mean 'travelled by the railway' is instanced in 1888: *Pall Mall Gazette,* 2 April, p. 4 col. 2: 'So exhausted were the men from the previous day's ride ... that all trained from Winchester to Farnham,' and *Harper's Magazine,* November 1888, p. 954 col. 2: 'From Aberdeen to Edinburgh we trained it in easy stages.' *OED.*

[102] One shilling for tea (including food) would be about £5.25 today; 3d for a cup of tea would be about £1.35.

[103] The Anglo-Boer Wars were fought in South Africa from 1880-1 and 1899-1902. With the British victory, the wars ended on 31 May 1902 on the signing of the Vereeniging Treaty, which ended the existence of the Transvaal and Orange Free State, which were placed in the British Empire. This cost the lives of 22,000 British troops and over 25,000 Boer civilians. The Boers were given £3 million in compensation and the promise of self-government in time. In 1910 the Union of South Africa was established. Thomas Pakenham, *The Boer War* (London: Abacus, 1991).

[104] General Piet (Pieter) Cronje (1836-1911) was born in Cape Colony, but raised in the South African Republic and became a General in the Boer forces. During the Second Boer War he laid siege to Kimberley and Mafeking, but he failed to prevent the British relief of Kimberley under Field Marshal Frederick Roberts and began to retreat. He reached the Modder River at Paardeberg, where he was surrounded but in the ensuing battle inflicted heavy losses on the British, who were commanded by Herbert Kitchener (320 dead and 942 wounded – the single costliest action of the war). However, besieged and attacked by Roberts' forces, who were helped by the Royal Canadian regiment, Cronje was forced to surrender, along with 4,019 men, who were taken prisoner, marching in a huge column – a spectacular sight. He himself was imprisoned with his wife on St. Helena Island until the end of hostilities. *Encyclopedia Britannica.*

[105] See John Bunyan's *The Pilgrim's Progress* (1678). Vanity Fair is so named because 'all that is there sold, or that cometh hither, is vanity'.

[106] This phrase echoes the children's Bible song, probably well-known to FCD: 'O be careful little eyes, what you see, for the Father up above is looking down in love ...', website: childbiblesongs.com/song-12-be-careful-little-eyes.shtml [accessed 28.11.15]

[107] Pleasant Sunday Afternoon (see Diary n. 54 on 24 August).

[108] Rusholme PM church in Monmouth Street, opened in 1898 and was part of the Manchester VI (Great Western Street) Circuit. The church later moved to Claremont Road, but closed in 1965.

[109] Local paper from King's Lynn, his home town.

[110] Mark Walsh, the person with whom he lodged when he was attending King's Lynn Technical College. In the house at 123 Church Street, King's Lynn were Mark Walsh (59), a Provision Dealer, his wife Elizabeth (57), and a niece, Gertrude (26), as well as FCD as a boarder. 1901 Census.

[111] These would be flowers that had been dried and pressed, a practice common in late Victorian and Edwardian times.

[112] Hebrews 4:16.

[113] Probably Philip A. Evans, a fellow-student, who went into circuit at Kingston in 1903 and then served in Brixton, Soham, Ludlow and Macclesfield. There is no further information after 1918. Leary, *Primitive Methodist Ministers*, p. 68.

[114] Probably David Cooke (1878-1957, see Diary n. 49 on 19 August).

[115] See Diary n. 18.

[116] The Free Trade Hall was named after an important principle. It stands on the site of the Peterloo massacre of 1819, when 60,000 people protesting about their lack of parliamentary representation were attacked by armed forces and 15 died. There were two halls, the large one seating 4,600 and the lesser hall accommodating 600. Schofield, *Manchester Then and Now*, p. 81.

[117] Travelling showmen had entertained in both Free Trade Halls for some years, but in May 1896 the cinematograph made its appearance in the Lesser Hall for a two-week visit. There were shows every half an hour and admission was 1 shilling. A series of photographs taken one after another were passed through a lantern slide projector in rapid succession, so that the division between each picture was imperceptible to the viewer who saw men and women moving as though alive. Soon showmen were adding cinematograph to their programme. 'Harry H. Hamilton's Excursions' had a show from 1880 entitled 'Round the Globe in 120 minutes,' which took the

audience from Charing Cross to China via Paris, the St. Gothard Tunnel, Venice, Mauritius, Egypt, India, Burma, San Francisco and New York, returning to Liverpool. There were scenes from the Afghan War, including the bombardment and capture of Kabul by British troops. A compère explained the action, and music and variety turns were used to break up the performance. From 1901 Hamilton added 'the most perfect animated picture projector ever invented' to his show. William Shenton, 'Manchester's First Cinemas', website: www.hssr.mmu.ac.uk [accessed 14.09.15].

[118] The impression of motion. Initially films were little more than views and brief jokes, but after 1900 they became longer and more ambitious. In 1901 an audience could expect to see a programme of about fifteen minutes on one reel, mostly news footage, with perhaps one or two fictional subjects. Shenton, 'Manchester's First Cinemas'.

[119] King Edward VII's coronation, on 9 August 1902 (see Diary n. 20) would be a topical attraction. The French stage magician Georges Melies produced a re-creation of this occasion. Shenton, 'Manchester's First Cinemas'.

[120] The Preston Guild was a massive celebration with processions and entertainments, which still takes place every twenty years. One of the years for the Guild would have been 1902. Preston was granted the right to have a Guild Merchant by Henry II in 1179 and the town was awarded its first royal charter. The Guild was an organisation of traders, craftsmen and merchants, who had a monopoly of trade in the town. Gatherings for renewing membership only happened infrequently, and it was accepted that they were only required once in a generation. Therefore from 1542 Preston Guild took place every 20 years. The rarity of the event and the fact that large numbers congregated in Preston for the occasion made the Guild a special opportunity for feasting, processions and great social gatherings. In 1790 there was freedom to trade in the town, which abolished the need for the Guild; however people continued to celebrate the Guild as its festivities had developed into prestigious social occasions. Website: www.preston.gov.uk/yourservices/events/preston-guild/guild-history [accessed 14.09.15]

[121] On 12 July 1902 a film was made of General Kitchener's arrival in Southampton at the end of the Boer War. He rode through decorated streets with General French in an open carriage. He had signed the treaty of Vereeniging following the Boers' surrender on 3 May 1902. Website: www.angloboerwar.com/forum/11-research/4591-films-about-the-boer-war [accessed 14.09.15].

[122] John Norton (1880-1967) was a student at the college. See Introduction n. 20, for details of his life.

[123] John 15:5.

[124] See Diary n. 54.

[125] See Diary n. 77, on 4 September, for the building. The Police Courts Mission in Manchester fulfilled the role that would be occupied by probation officers in modern times. The *Guardian* newspaper, 2 May 2007, gives a history of the Probation Service, which arose from the Church of England Temperance Society appointing two 'missionaries' to Southwark Crown Court, initially to 'reclaim drunkards'. This was the basis for the setting up of the London Police Courts Mission, whose missionaries worked with magistrates to develop a system of releasing offenders on condition that they kept in touch with the missionary and accepted guidance. In 1886 The Probation of First Time Offenders Act allowed courts around the country to follow the London example of appointing missionaries and evidently Manchester was one of the few cities that actually did. Not until 1907 were these missionaries given status as 'officers of the court', later known as probation officers. The *Guardian* (9 October 2004) quotes an article of 5 September 1890 reporting on a letter written by Miss Florence Nightingale to Mr Alex Devine of the Gordon Boys' Home and the Mission to Lads at the Police Courts, on the subject of juvenile offenders. Miss Nightingale writes, 'The work you are doing at Manchester in rescuing boys 'had up' for their first offence is one of overwhelming importance, and yours is, as far as I know, the first and only one of its kind.' She goes on to describe how the Mission, 'profiting from the First Offenders Act', attends the Police Courts and offers the magistrate the means of carrying out the Act successfully. She suggests that, instead of sending the offender to prison – supported by the rates – he should be made to work out the price of what he stole and that experience sadly proves that gaol is not a deterrent. W. McWilliams, 'The Mission to the Police Courts 1876-1936', *The Howard Journal* 22 (1983) pp. 129-47.

[126] The penalties for crimes are confirmed by the British Transport Police website e.g. on 28 May 1881 William Klingender received six months imprisonment with hard labour for stealing a bag at Manchester Victoria Station. www.btp.police.uk [accessed 12.11.14].

[127] Peter Taylor Forsyth (1848-1921), Congregational minister, was born in Aberdeen, the son of a postman who was also a deacon in the Congregational Church. He was educated at Aberdeen University where he obtained a first-class degree in Classics and later in Germany, under Albrecht Ritschl in Göttingen. On his return he entered New College,

London. He held four pastorates, Shipley, Yorks. (1876-9), Cheetham Hill, Manchester (1885-8), Clarendon Park, Leicester (1888-94) and Emmanuel Church Cambridge (1894-1901), before becoming Principal of Hackney College in 1901, where he remained until his death. He wrote 25 books, and was considered one of the most outstanding theologians of his generation. Central to his preaching was the great stress he laid on the Atonement. For him the cross was the central fact of Christianity, round which everything else centred. *Congregational Year Book, 1922*. Leslie McCurdy, *Attribute and Atonement: The Holy Love of God in the Theology of P. T. Forsyth* (Carlisle: Paternoster, 1998).

[128] Chorlton Road Congregational Chapel (see Diary n. 80).

[129] Christian Endeavour (see Diary n. 72).

[130] William Hughes (1870-1958) was a student in FCD's year at college. Born at Pennerley, Shropshire, he moved with his parents to Wales when he was thirteen. He entered the college in 1902, then went into circuit in Sheffield as a probationary minister in 1904. He served in seven other circuits, Leicester IV, Leicester II, Ashby de la Zouch, Rugby, Coventry (Paradise), Hasbury and Cromer, before retiring to Cromer in 1952, where he continued to preach. *Minutes of Conference 1959*, p. 177; Leary, *Primitive Methodist Ministers*, p. 109.

[131] See Introduction pp. 25-8.

[132] See Diary n. 29 on 11 August.

[133] Andrew Martin Fairbairn, (1838-1912) was Principal of Mansfield College from 1886 until 1909 (see Introduction p. 16). Born near Edinburgh, he entered the Congregational ministry, holding pastorates at Bathgate, West Lothian and at Aberdeen, and was principal of Airedale College, Bradford (1877-86). But it was as the first principal of Mansfield College, Oxford, that he exercised most influence, not only over generations of his own students, but also over a large number of undergraduates in the university generally. In 1883 he was chairman of the Congregational Union of England and Wales and a member of the Royal Commission on Secondary Education in 1894-95. He was a prolific writer on theological subjects. William Boothby Selbie, *Life of Andrew Martin Fairbairn* (London: Hodder & Stoughton, 1914).

[134] James Hope Moulton (1863-1917) was from a well-known Wesleyan family, a brilliant classicist and the first Nonconformist minister to be elected fellow of a Cambridge college (King's). He won fame as a philologist, becoming the greatest English authority on Zoroastrianism.

With Deissman and Milligan, he applied new evidence from papyri to the interpretation of New Testament Greek. In 1902 he was appointed Tutor in NT Language and Literature at Didsbury College and also became Greenwood Professor of Hellenistic Greek at Manchester University. In 1915 he went to India to lecture on Zoroaster. When the ship on which he was returning from India was torpedoed in 1917, after three stormy days in an open boat, he died of exposure and was buried at sea, aged fifty-three. *Minutes of Conference 1917*; *Dictionary of Methodism*, p. 247.

[135] William John Townsend (1835-1915) was a United Methodist minister, who was President of the National Free Church Council in 1902. He was a powerful and enthusiastic preacher, serving in various circuits, from Ladywood, Birmingham to Forest Hill, London, but the longest period was in Halifax, 1869-1879. He was President of the Methodist New Connexion in 1886 and President of the UM Church in 1908, the first complete year of its existence. He was a great advocate of Union and wrote *The Story of Methodist Union*, and he was one of the editors of the *New History of Methodism* (1909). *United Methodist Church Minutes of Conference 1915*; *Dictionary of Methodism*, p. 356.

[136] Alexander MacKennal (1835-1904) was minister of Bowdon Downs Congregational Church between 1876 and 1904, a prosperous church on the southern edge of Manchester. He was a leading intellectual and opinion-former among the ministers of the day. In 1887 he was Chair of the Congregational Union, and it was he who established the International Congregational Council. Bebbington, *The Nonconformist Conscience*, pp. 63-4; *Congregational Yearbook 1905*.

[137] About £4 in today's money.

[138] Luke 22:19.

[139] It is uncertain who this is. It sounds like a fellow-student, and there is a Frank Jones listed as a first-year student at the College in 1902, but there is no trace of him in Leary, *PM Ministers,* nor in *Who's Who in Methodism 1933*.

[140] This was an interesting social occasion, which evidently fell into disuse as fruit became more widely available and less of a luxury.

[141] Robert Burns (1759-96), Scottish poet, whose romantic and sometimes sentimental poetry appealed to Victorians and retains its attraction today. He was an inspiration to those of liberal and socialist outlook; he understood the character of his nation and was known for his humanity. Ian McIntyre, *Robert Burns: A Life* (London: Constable, 2009).

[142] Thomas Alfred Fairweather (1879-1948) was born at Scarborough and after studying at Hartley he went to his first circuit appointment in St. Neots in 1903. His ministry over forty years was largely in busy towns and cities: Biggleswade, Hastings, Liverpool III, Douglas, Hull III, Leeds II, Liverpool II, Bradford VI, Shipley, Batley and Birkenshaw. He was a wise administrator and for twelve years served as Secretary of the Bradford District. *Minutes of Conference 1949*; Leary, *Primitive Methodist Ministers.*

[143] Alderman Thomas Beeley JP (1833-1908) was appointed treasurer of the college in 1887. He held office until his death in 1908, when he was succeeded by his son, T. Carter Beeley, (1869-1909) who only held office for a year before he too died. Thomas Beeley was the owner of the firm Thomas Beeley & Son, Boilermakers, of Hyde Junction Iron Works, a company he founded himself in 1865 and which, by 1871 was employing 130 men and boys. His son, Thomas Carter Beeley, took over the management of the firm in 1890. Thomas Beeley married Elizabeth Carter and the family lived at Pole Bank Hall, Hyde. 1871 census; website: www.gracesguide.co.uk/Thomas_Beeley_and_Son [accessed 6.2.15].

[144] Woodley railway station is situated nine and a quarter miles east of Manchester Piccadilly on the Great Central line. From there it is about half a mile's walk to Pole Bank House.

[145] The word means that they caused mist and no doubt pollution in the atmosphere.

[146] Note the use of this word – we would probably have said 'spreads'.

[147] A 1904 Board of Trade report of the cost of food for 2,000 working families suggests that the normal pattern was four meals a day: Breakfast, quite often including bacon or egg; Dinner, meat, potatoes, sometimes with other vegetables and sometimes pudding; Tea, bread and butter, sometimes with egg or cold meat, and cake; Supper, a range of foods such as kippers, bacon, fish, cold meat, or porridge, with bread and butter and a hot drink. John Burnett, *A History of the Cost of Living* (London: Penguin, 1965), pp. 269-72.

[148] Ernest Edward Fisher was a close friend in college (see Diary n. 18).

[149] Oswald Edward Brown (1881-1972) was born at Monkwearmouth, County Durham and after leaving school worked in a shipping office in Sunderland. Four of his brothers were ministers. After training at Hartley, he served in the following circuits: Dalton & Millom, Malton, Lowestoft, Clay Cross, Derby IV, Bath, Pontypool, Brierley Hill, Oswestry Chapel St., Chesterfield Salter, and Belper before retiring to Derby in 1948. *Minutes of Conference 1973*; Leary, *Primitive Methodist Ministers.*

[150] See Introduction pp. 25-8.

[151] The central square in Manchester. After Prince Albert's early death in 1861, the public space was named in his honour. Albert was much loved in Manchester for his belief in progress, education and commerce. A striking memorial was erected in the square in 1867, designed by Thomas Worthington and containing a statue of the Prince by Matthew Noble. A memorial hall designed by Worthington in the Venetian style was built, extending along the south side of the square. On the eastern side is the magnificent Town Hall. Cecil Steward, *The Stones of Manchester* (London: Edward Arnold, 1956); Schofield, *Manchester Then and Now.*

[152] Alfred Eddison Hutton MP (1865-1947) was a Liberal politician and manufacturer. He came from Eccleshill, near Bradford, where he lived most of his life. In 1892 he was elected Liberal MP for Morley in the West Riding of Yorkshire. *Debrett's House of Commons 1901.*

[153] Henry Broadhurst MP (1840-1911) was a leading early trade unionist and a Lib-Lab politician who sat variously in the House of Commons between 1885 and 1906. He entered politics as MP for Stoke-on-Trent in 1880. A leading campaigner for the extension of the franchise and the rights of working men, he was secretary of the TUC Parliamentary Committee. Five years later, he was elected MP for Birmingham Bordesley and was appointed Under-secretary for State for the Home Department in the Liberal government, the first person from a working-class background to hold a ministerial position. He became MP for Nottingham West in 1886, but lost the seat in 1892. Then in 1894 he was elected MP for Leicester at a by-election, holding the seat as a Lib-Lab MP until 1906. He was a powerful figure with a strong voice, outspoken and a leading figure in the labour movement in its early days. J. R. MacDonald and Marc Brodie, in *ODNB.*

[154] Samuel Chadwick (1860-1932) was a Wesleyan Methodist minister and a leading evangelical preacher of his day, closely associated with the holiness tradition and zeal for social action. He had a notable ministry at Oxford Place in the Leeds Mission (1894-1907), during which he brought about revival; he would contend with atheists and agnostics in the Town Square and many were converted. After this, in 1907, he became Tutor and then Principal of Cliff College, where he stayed for 25 years, training evangelists and creating the 'Cliff spirit'. He was Chairman of the Sheffield District 1911-26 and President of the Wesleyan Methodist Conference in 1918 and later President of the National Council of Evangelical Free Churches. He was editor of *Joyful News*, where much of

his writing is to be found. *Minutes of Conference 1933*; *Dictionary of Methodism*, p. 58.

[155] J. E. Roberts was junior or co-pastor at Union Chapel (see Diary n. 57 on 24 August).

[156] Robert Hind (1851-1909) went to the York Circuit in 1900. He was born at Nenthead, high in the Pennine hills, and showed intellectual ability from an early age. He was also tall and strong, and able to do a man's work at 15. He became a preacher at the age of 16, and after being recommended for the ministry he spent a year at the Sunderland Institute, before his probationary appointment at Crook. He then served in the following circuits: Blyth, Gateshead, Durham, Paisley, Middlesbrough and York. During his six years in Middlesbrough, a great revival was experienced. He was also active in public life, on the school board and President of the Free Church Council. Many were shocked by his early death in Newcastle, where he had gone to seek treatment from a surgeon. *PM Magazine, 1909*; Leary, *Primitive Methodist Ministers.*

[157] Benjamin Aquila Barber (1876-1946) was born in Leeds into a respected and influential Primitive Methodist family. He candidated for the ministry and entered Hartley in 1897. Then in 1899 he went to the Tunstall Circuit, where he stayed until 1904. After that he served in the following circuits and appointments: Spennymoor, Bishop Auckland, 1912-1920 Chaplain to HM Forces, Newcastle III, Harrogate, 1931-5 Connexional Editor, Lytham St. Annes, Lancaster and Aireborough. He died within a few weeks of his retirement. *Minutes of Conference 1947*; Leary, *Primitive Methodist Ministers.*

[158] Arthur Beavan (1850-1922) was a PM minister in the Manchester circuits between 1901 and 1908. He was born at Dulas in Herefordshire; his father died when he was a child, but his mother, an intensely religious woman, was an abiding influence on his life. He committed his life to Christ at such a young age that class leaders doubted he could understand what it meant and, when he became a preacher shortly after, he was dubbed the 'boy preacher'. He entered the ministry in 1871 and spent 47 years in the active work. Even after superannuating in 1918, he took charge of the church at Eastbourne on the death of its minister, then in 1921 he undertook the superintendency of the Horsham Circuit. Sadly, that autumn, his health failed and he died the following February. He served in the following circuits: Swansea, Bristol, Bath, Pontypool, Radstock, Blaenavon, Darlaston, Reading, Luton I, Hull III, Matlock, Manchester III, Manchester IX, Ossett, Manchester XI, Northampton, Fulham, Eastbourne and Horsham. He was a member of the Hartley College Committee for several years and in 1912 the

Secretary of the PM Conference. Leary, *Primitive Methodist Ministers*; *PM Magazine*, 1922.

[159] The United Kingdom Alliance (UKA) was the main political arm of the temperance movement. It was founded in 1853 in Manchester after a meeting called by Nathaniel Caird (1805-56), an Irish cotton manufacturer and member of the Society of Friends. He had been a member of the Manchester and Salford Temperance Society and now formed a group to work for the prohibition of the trade in alcohol in Britain, following the example of General Neal Dow's law in Maine, USA in 1851 prohibiting the sale of intoxicants. The UKA's members were prohibitionists, who felt that the individual's liberty had to come second to the over-riding duty to eliminate the evil of drink. Its members were mostly Nonconformists, and this was one manifestation of the 'Nonconformist Conscience' behind the moral crusades of the time. A. E. Dingle, *The Campaign for Prohibition in Victorian England* (London: Croom Helm, 1980).

[160] Arthur James Balfour, First Earl of Balfour (1848-1930), was Prime Minister from 1902 until 1906, during which time the Education Act was passed (see Introduction). He entered Parliament in 1874 as Conservative member for Hertford and from 1885 he served as MP for Manchester East, a seat he held until 1906. On 12 July 1902 he became Prime Minister. He later served under Lloyd George as Foreign Secretary, and was responsible for the famous Balfour Declaration (1917), which promised Zionists a national home in Palestine. Max Egremont, *Balfour: A Life of Arthur James Balfour* (London: Weidenfeld and Nicolson, 1998).

[161] Sir Wilfrid Lawson (1829-1906), second baronet, is probably meant, rather than his younger brother William, who was an agriculturist involved in the Co-operative movement. Sir Wilfrid Lawson was an Anglican of evangelical background, and a temperance campaigner who in 1879 became President of the United Kingdom Alliance. He was a radical, anti-imperialist Liberal Party politician, who was the MP for Carlisle, Cockermouth and Camborne at various times over the period 1859-1906 He repeatedly during the nineteenth century tried to introduce to Parliament a bill which would permit localities to prohibit the sale of alcohol. By the time of his death, however, his approach to temperance reform had lost much of its support and most reformers doubted that parliament could be persuaded to enact the 'local veto' on the drink trade. G. W. E. Russell, revised by David M. Fahey, in *ODNB*.

[162] Leif (Leifchild) Jones (1862-1939) was the son of Thomas Jones, the Poet-Preacher of Wales and chair of the Congregational Union of England and

Wales. He was educated in Melbourne, Australia, where his father was working, and Trinity College, Oxford, and contested several seats, including South Manchester in 1900, before being elected MP for North Westmoreland in 1906. In 1910 he became MP for Rushcliffe, Notts, then 1923-4 and 1929-31 for Camborne. He was a member of the United Kingdom Temperance Alliance, becoming their President from 1906-1932 and frequently appeared on temperance platforms, being popularly referred to as 'Tea-leaf Jones'. G. B. Wilson, *Leif Jones, Lord Rhyader: Temperance Reformer and Statesman* (Birmingham: United Kingdom Alliance, 1948).

[163] Canon Edward Lee Hicks (1843-1919) was an eminent Anglican priest, scholar and a social reformer. Educated at Magdalen College School and Brasenose College Oxford, he was ordained in 1886. After a time as Fellow and Tutor of Corpus Christi College, Oxford, he was Rector of Fenny Compton before becoming the first principal of Hulme Hall. After this, he was Canon Residentiary at Manchester Cathedral, then Rural Dean of Salford, before becoming Bishop of Lincoln in 1910, where he remained until his death in 1919. He became a teetotaller in 1877, influenced by the working men's temperance society set up in Fenny Compton and for the rest of his life was a tireless campaigner for temperance reform. He wrote for the *Alliance News* and from 1904 for the *Manchester Guardian*, and addressed many temperance meetings. When accused by a heckler of 'trying to rob the poor man of his beer', he replied that he was trying to prevent beer robbing the poor man. M. C. Curthoys, in *ODNB*.

[164] Thomas Palmer Whittaker (1850-1919) was the Liberal MP for Spen Valley, in the West Riding of Yorkshire. He was born in Scarborough, and went into business at the age of sixteen. In 1882 he became editor of a number of newspapers and moved to London. He was elected to Parliament in 1882 and held the seat until his death. In Parliament he was an advocate of the temperance movement and sought reform of the alcohol licensing laws.

[165] William Wightman of the Progressive Party was elected to the London County Council on 2 March 1901, to represent Lambeth North. The Progressive Party was founded in 1888 by a group of Liberals and leaders of the Labour movement. In the first elections of the London City Council in 1889, the Progressive Party won 70 of the 118 seats. It lost power in 1907 to the Municipal Reform Party (a conservative organization). Website [accessed 14.11.14]: https://en.wikipedia.org/wiki/List_of_members_of_London_County_Council_1889–1919.

[166] Silas Hocking (1850-1935) was a Cornish minister in the United Methodist Free Church. He had a popular ministry in Southport (1883-96), before devoting himself to writing and Liberal politics. He resigned from the ministry in 1906. He wrote nearly 100 novels and an autobiography. Roger F. S. Thorne, in *Dictionary of Methodism*, p. 160.

[167] Leonard Monk Isitt (1854-1937), a Methodist minister, temperance leader and politician in New Zealand, was on one of his four speaking tours to England at the invitation of the United Kingdom Alliance. He was born in Bedford, England, then as a young man joined his brother in New Zealand, felt called to the ministry and was ordained in 1881. An incident where he was called upon to conduct the burial of a man who had died of alcoholic poisoning, whose body was hurried by a drunken driver to a grave half-dug by a drunken grave-digger, had a profound effect on him and he set his whole energies to fight the evil of alcohol. He was stationed at Auckland, Marsterton, Wellington, Christchurch and Sydenham (New Zealand), a working-class area where the problem of drink was only too apparent. He started a paper 'The Prohibitionist', and embarked on a speaking campaign, so effective that the Methodist Conference released him from his ordinary work. He also tried to gain control of the Licensing Committee and refuse licences to all hotels in the area, but was defeated in the courts by the publicans. George Ranald Macdonald, in *An Encyclopedia of New Zealand*, ed. A. H. McLintock (Wellington NZ: Owen, Govt. Printer, 1966).

[168] This was an enormous sum at a time when a working man's wage might be less than than £1 a week. An inflation calculator gives a current value as about £321,960.

[169] See Introduction p. 25 regarding the Education Bill and the massive protests against it by Nonconformists. His speech of 14 October 1902, alluded to here, is reported in *The Times* of 15 October: 'Why, people had asked, had the government decided to disturb the "social peace" with this measure? The answer is this, that the existing education system of this country is chaotic, is ineffectual, is utterly behind the age, makes us the laughing-stock of every advanced nation in Europe and America and it was not consistent with the duty of an English government – of a British government – to allow that state of things longer to continue.' *ODNB*.

[170] St. James's Church was on the north side of Charlotte Street. It was consecrated in 1786 and demolished in 1928. St. James House was built on the site. Presumably St. James's Hall was associated with this church, which was still standing in 1902. Hartwell, *Manchester*, p. 150.

[171] FCD had an interest in photography, evident from comments on postcards to and from his brother Cecil on the subject. Many Methodist ministers had their photographs taken, and these could be used in publicity for events in which they were taking part. Postcards were made of the photographs of leading ministers, as are listed in Tom Norgate's book on the life of John William Righton (1857-1921), a Wesleyan schoolteacher turned photographer. Tom Norgate, *From Pedagogy to Photography* (Petersfield: 613 Books, 2008), pp. 93-4, 101-29.

[172] One shilling and three pence, which would be about £6.70 today.

[173] Presumably a reference to Adam Clarke's eight-volume commentary on the Bible, which was begun in May 1798 and completed in March 1825. Adam Clarke (*c.* 1760-1832) was prominent in Methodist circles after John Wesley's death and involved in various controversies, but his lasting legacy was his academic work. After learning Hebrew in his first circuit, he progressed to Syriac, Arabic, Persian, Ethiopian and Coptic. His time in London was extended so that the Bible Society could use his gifts. He served as President of Conference three times (1806, 1814 and 1822). Although a prolific author, his Bible commentary was the most significant, demonstrating not only his knowledge of Bible languages, but his critical acumen, producing conclusions ahead of his time. There was controversy over his unorthodox views on the eternal sonship of Christ, and Richard Watson (1781-1833) suggested that his rationalist principles of interpretation were capable of Arian and Socinian developments in the hands of less reliable exegetes. He died of cholera in London in 1832 and is buried close to John Wesley at Wesley's Chapel. Martin Wellings, 'Adam Clarke', in *BDE*, pp.144-6; N. W. Taggart, in *Dictionary of Methodism in Britain and Ireland*, p. 69.

[174] See Diary n. 54.

[175] Presumably to Withington, to Charlie Wright's house again.

[176] Mark Guy Pearse (1842-1930) was a Wesleyan Methodist minister and prolific author. Born in Camborne, his writings reflect his lifelong devotion to his native Cornwall. He became a medical student in 1861, but the call to the ministry led him to enter Didsbury College in 1862. In 1863 he was stationed in Leeds and continued with growing popularity in various circuits. Then, from 1887 until 1904, he was a colleague of Hugh Price Hughes at the West London Mission where he did invaluable work for seventeen years. When he preached his first sermon at St. James' Hall in 1887, 1,000 people gathered to hear him. *Minutes of Conference 1930*; Mrs George Unwin and John Telford, *Mark Guy Pearse* (London: Epworth Press, 1930).

[177] See Introduction pp. 19-20 and Diary n. 47 on 19 August.

[178] For many people, the most significant verse in the Bible: 'For God so loved the world that he gave his only begotten Son, that whosoever believeth in him should not perish, but have everlasting life.'

[179] Ignacy Jan Paderewski (1860-1941) was born in Kurylowka, Poland. His early years were spent with his father, a land-agent, and sister, moving to an aunt's house when his father was arrested. He was mostly self-taught, but in 1872, at the age of twelve, he was admitted to the Warsaw Conservatory. After graduating in 1878, he travelled to Berlin, where he met Richard Strauss and Anton Rubinstein, and Vienna, where he took lessons from Leschetizky. He taught in Strasbourg and Paris and his success there led to concert tours throughout Europe and America. As well as being a brilliant pianist, he was active politically and, upon Poland achieving independence in 1917, became the country's first Prime Minister and Minister of Foreign Affairs. Stanley Sadie (ed.), *The New Grove Dictionary of Music and Musicians* 2nd edition (London: Macmillan, 2001).

[180] Presumably the nickname of his college, as being near Alexandra Park. It was not named 'Hartley' until 1906. See Introduction pp. 11-12.

[181] Bolton was a town about twelve miles north-west of Manchester, where the cotton textile industry flourished. In 1902 large mills would have dominated the skyline; by 1911, 36,000 people were employed in the industry. After 1920 decline set in with the fall in cotton prices. Website: www.bolton.org [accessed 19.11.14].

[182] Halliwell PM Chapel was about a mile and a half from the station, to the north-west of the town centre. It is closed today.

[183] This would be travelling on the Lancashire & Yorkshire Railway.

[184] When the Primitive Methodist Connexion celebrated its Jubilee in 1860 (50 years after the first class meeting in 1810), it was decided that part of the Jubilee Fund be devoted to establishing a mission in Southern Africa. In 1870 a station was opened 300 miles from the coast on the Orange River. When a young minister was requested, Rev. Henry Buckenham was sent, later joined by John Smith. Ill-health forced Buckenham's return to England and his first wife died on the journey home, but after re-marrying, he set out again in 1889 with two colleagues, one of whom was Rev Arthur Baldwin, this time to mission to the Ila people, north of the Zambezi. John Pritchard, *Methodists and their Missionary Societies 1760-1900* (Farnham: Ashgate, 2013), p. 190.

[185] Arthur Baldwin, FRGS, (1864-1937), was born in Otley, Yorkshire, into a Methodist family and educated at Otley Collegiate School. He entered the Primitive Methodist ministry in 1887 in Barrowford, then moved to Halifax for a year, and then joined a pioneer party led by Henry Buckenham, sent out by the Primitive Methodist Missionary Committee to establish mission centres in South Central Africa. They sailed on 24 April 1889. They were to explore an area of the Zambezi that no white man had previously penetrated. Nkala was reached four years later and a mission established. The journey was one of extreme peril, hardship and deprivation; it is recorded that to cross the Zambezi, which was over half a mile wide, they had to float the wagons across, the oxen swam over and the goods were ferried over in dug-out canoes. However, once they arrived, their work formed a sound basis for extensive missionary development in subsequent years. Arthur Baldwin was working in the area of the Zambezi until 1895, then at Mashakulum for a year, and from 1896 until 1902 in Nkala. After 13 years in Africa, he had to return home on health grounds and was stationed in Halifax, but he continued an impressive and convincing advocacy of the missionary task. So in this instance he had been invited over as a newly returned missionary to tell of his experiences. On his return to the home work he served in the following circuits: Halifax, Brighouse, Nottingham IV, Gainsborough, Leeds VIII; from 1919-1924 he was Missionary Finance Secretary; he was also Secretary of the insurance Company and Chapel Aid Association. He then served for a year in Kingston before becoming secretary of Christian Aid from 1925 until his retirement in York in 1936. He died a year later, having lived his whole life faithfully in the service of the Lord and taking the message to those who, in the words of John Wesley, 'need it most'. *Minutes of Conference 1938*; Pritchard, *Methodists and their Missionary Societies*, p.190; Arthur Baldwin, *A Missionary Outpost in Central Africa: The Story of the Baila Mission* (London: W. A. Hammond, Primitive Methodist House, 1928).

[186] This is spelt Mashukulumbwe in the obituary of Henry Buckenham. *PM Minutes of Conference 1897.*

[187] King's Lynn.

[188] It is not certain who is referred to here, but it may be Henry Buckenham's second wife (his first wife, Maria, having died on the way home from a previous missionary expedition to Africa). The wives of missionaries were commonly referred to as 'Sister'. However, as this wife is always spoken of in reports and obituaries as 'Mrs Buckenham', it is not possible to be sure. Their small daughter, who sadly died on the arduous journey in Africa, was called Elsie, which might suggest that Mrs Buckenham was

called Elsie and her daughter named after her. Henry Buckenham came from Fakenham in Norfolk, where the present Methodist Church is known as the Henry Buckenham Memorial Church, so the family may well have been known in King's Lynn and to FCD.

[189] Perhaps 'lumping'.

[190] Great Western Street PM Chapel (see Diary n. 46).

[191] Evidently he was referred to as 'professor' even though he was first appointed to a chair at the university only in 1904.

[192] Luke 22:19

[193] John Gershom Greenhough (1843-1933), a Baptist minister, was born in Germany, but came to England very soon afterwards and lived in Yorkshire where his family settled. After having to leave school at the age of eleven, he worked at a saddler's and saved his money to buy books. He was accepted for training at Rawdon College and obtained the BA and MA degrees at London University. He went as minister to Coseley, then Cotham Grove Baptist Chapel in Bristol, where he was also tutor and secretary of the Bristol Baptist College. He then took over the pastorate of Victoria Road, Leicester Baptist Chapel at a difficult time, when there had been a split in the congregation, after the previous minister, Rev. F. B. Meyer had set up another chapel (Melbourne Hall) nearby, and taken a portion of the congregation with him. John Greenhough followed a peaceable course, remaining on good terms with Meyer, and by diligent visiting and effective preaching held the congregation together and stayed 25 years. He was not afraid to say to the well-off members of his congregation that he wanted to make Leicester a place where the rich help the poor and the poor love the great, a city where love, charity and brotherhood reign supreme. He became a national figure as well as a local celebrity, and was President of the Baptist Missionary Society, the Baptist Union in 1895 and the National Free Church Council in 1901. J. E. Greenhough, *The Cross in Modern Life* (London: Hodder and Stoughton, 1896), pp. 46-53; Gerald Rimmington, 'Victoria Road Church, Leicester – a Victorian Experiment in Ecumenicity', *Transactions of the Leicestershire Archaeological and Historical Society* 71 (1997), pp. 80-85; some information supplied by Emily Burgoyne, Librarian, Regent's Park College.

[194] Phil. 2:9-10a.

[195] Methodist Central Hall in Oldham Street. The first Methodist chapel in Oldham Street had been opened by John Wesley in 1781. A hundred years later, this area of Manchester was very different; the middle classes had moved

to the suburbs, leaving the poor working classes. In the 1880s, in response to the desperate plight of the urban poor, the Forward Movement was set up in Wesleyan Methodism by Hugh Price Hughes in London and H. P. Pope in Manchester, one feature of which was the building of Central Halls. These were multi-purpose buildings, with the worship area more like a theatre, blurring the distinction between ecclesiastical and secular to make the ordinary working-class person feel more at home. So in Oldham Street, the chapel was pulled down and Central Hall Mission, the first of its kind, was opened in 1886. It became the headquarters of the Manchester and Salford Mission, and under the dynamic leadership of Samuel Collier was very successful. Sunday service congregations grew to be too large to be accommodated, so services were held in the Free Trade Hall, resulting in some of the largest Methodist congregations anywhere. *Dictionary of Methodism*, pp. 126, 221.

[196] Hugh Black (1868-1953) was a Scottish-American theologian and author. He was born in Rothesay, Scotland, and received an MA degree from Glasgow University in 1887. He then studied Divinity at the Free Church College, Glasgow, 1887-91 and was ordained in 1891. He began his work in Glasgow, as assistant to Ross Taylor, and then soon after moved to Sherwood Free Church, Paisley. People were impressed by his forceful preaching and he became Associate Pastor at St. George's Free Presbyterian Church in Edinburgh in 1896. As he became widely known, invitations poured in to preach on special occasions in London and other large cities. He emigrated to the United States in 1906 to accept the post of Chair of Practical Theology at Union Theological Seminary in New York City. He later accepted the position of pastor of the First Congregational Church in Montclair, New Jersey, and retired in 1938. He was the author of numerous books, from *Friendship* (1898) to *Christ or Caesar* (1936). Website: www.electricscotland.com/history/descendants/chap38htm, [accessed on 27.10.2014].

[197] Numbers 10:29b.

[198] Later to become the University of Manchester (See Diary n. 31).

[199] Samuel Francis Collier (1855-1921), Wesleyan minister and founder of the Manchester and Salford Mission in 1886, was born in Runcorn and made the decision for Christ at Trinity Chapel, Southport at the age of sixteen. He offered for the ministry and in 1877 entered Didsbury College. After a year serving in Kent and three in Brentford, in 1877 he was appointed to the Oldham Street congregation in Manchester, while the Central Hall was being built. His frank, direct preaching drew numbers and a remarkable revival took place. In 1886 he entered upon the work of the Manchester Mission in

the new Central Hall. Under his leadership, with the combination of evangelism and social action, the membership of the Mission grew from 93 members in 1887 to 3,521 in 1902. The years of the First World War, when two of his sons were killed, were a time of strain and sorrow, but he struggled on to maintain the work of the Mission. He was the longest-serving of the 'great three' Missions' minsters, Rev. F. L. Wiseman and Rev. S. Chadwick being the other two, both great friends. After a delegation to Australia and New Zealand in 1920, he returned apparently revived, but his heart had been strained. He died in harness, while still Superintendent of the Manchester Mission, in 1921 at the age of sixty-five. On the day of his funeral, at which Wiseman and Chadwick spoke, the city streets were blocked with people who lined the pavements, to watch more than a hundred funeral cars make their way to the cemetery. *Minutes of Conference* 1921; *Dictionary of Methodism* p. 74; John Banks: *Samuel Francis Collier* (Peterborough: Foundery Press, 1996).

[200] John Shaw Banks (1835-1917), a Wesleyan minister, was born in Sheffield to Methodist parents, but brought up in Birmingham, where he attended King Edward's Grammar School. He felt called to preach at the age of 16 and was accepted for the ministry when he was 19 years old. After brief training, he was a pioneer missionary in the Mysore District of India 1856-65, then for 15 years he travelled in home circuits, ranging from Plymouth to Glasgow. In 1880 he was appointed to the Chair of Theology at Headingley College, Leeds, where he stayed for 30 years. For 23 years he was Chairman of the Leeds District, holding the confidence and affection of ministers and people alike. He was the President of the Wesleyan Methodist Conference in 1902, and his *Manual of Christian Doctrine* has been widely read. *Minutes of Conference* 1917.

[201] Arthur Tappan Pierson (1837-1911), an American Presbyterian minister, was a well-known evangelist who is said to have preached over 13,000 sermons, to have written over 50 books and also gave Bible lectures in a transatlantic ministry that made him famous. Born and educated in New York, he held pastorates in America from 1859 and then, when Charles Spurgeon became ill, he took over the work at the Metropolitan Tabernacle in London in 1891. He was best known for his advocacy of world evangelization and as a promoter of the holiness tradition associated with the Keswick Convention. From 1902-3 he was pastor at Christ Church in London. He edited the periodical *Missionary Review* for 25 years and was a consulting editor of the original *Scofield Reference Bible* (1909), a friend of Dwight Moody, and a fervent supporter of foreign missions and ecumenical action. *BDE* pp. 526-

8; Dana Robert, *Occupy till I Come: A. T. Pierson and the Evangelization of the World* (Grand Rapids, MI: Eerdmans, 2003).

[202] Samuel Chadwick (see Diary n. 154 on 11 October).

[203] Frederick Luke Wiseman (1858-1944), a Wesleyan minister, was born at York, the son of a minister. After being accepted for the ministry he trained at Didsbury and was later assistant tutor there. He spent the greater part of his ministry, twenty-six years, at the Birmingham Mission. He was President of the Wesleyan Methodist Church in 1912 and the Methodist Conference in 1933. He was a forceful evangelical preacher, sometimes breaking into song for the very joy of his message, and a strong advocate of Home Missions. He was chairman of the committee preparing the Methodist Hymn Book in 1933, which contained several tunes he had written himself, including the tune to 'Come let us sing of a wonderful love'. *Minutes of Conference, 1944.*

[204] John Duxbury, Professor of Elocution at Lancaster Independent College, was engaged by the Primitive Methodist College to take students for reading and exposition. He established the Manchester School of Elocution and was in 1908 appointed Director of Studies in Elocution at the Victoria University of Manchester. He gave performances all over the country and abroad. Website: digital.lib.uiowa.edu/cdm/ref/collection/tc/id/51115; sdrc.lib.uiowa.edu/traveling-culture/chau1/pdf/Duxbury/4/brochure.pdf, [accessed on 07.11.14].

[205] Not clear. Presumably 'Test Match'.

[206] Higher Broughton is an area north of Manchester city centre. There was a PM Chapel on Great Clowes Street, near the junction with Camp Street.

[207] Higher Broughton.

[208] John Harryman Taylor (1867-1931) was a minister in Manchester in 1902. He was born at Brompton, near Northallerton, the son of John Taylor, a PM minster, and educated at the Royal Grammar School, Newcastle and St. John's College, Cambridge. His first degree in 1889 was in mathematics. While an undergraduate, he began to preach and heard the call to the Christian ministry. He took a three-year postgraduate course in theology at Mansfield College, Oxford under Fairbairn. One of his tutors was A. S. Peake, who was introduced by him to W. P. Hartley and persuaded to move to the college at Manchester, with immeasurable benefits to ministerial education. His first appointment was in Reading, where he married Annie Harbottle, after which he served in the following circuits: Newcastle II, Manchester III (Great Clowes Street, 1902-5),

Manchester VI (Great Western Street), Matlock, Birkenhead, Northampton, Whitby and Saltburn, before retiring to Kendal in 1928. For many years he was secretary of the Probationers' Examining Committee and was appointed Director of the Insurance Company and Chapel Aid Association shortly before his death on 6 February 1931. *Primitive Methodist Magazine 1932.*

[209] See Diary n. 45.

[210] See 1 Kings 8:17-19: 'And it was in the heart of David my father to build an house for the name of the Lord God of Israel. And the Lord said unto David my father, Whereas it was in thine heart to build an house ... nevertheless thou shalt not build the house; but thine son ... shall build the house unto my name.'

[211] Space left blank.

[212] William George Softley (1870-1949, see Introduction n. 66 for details of his life).

[213] Charlie Wright, who has previously entertained him at Withington.

[214] The word is not easy to read. It may be a French term for a period of work, linked to 'seminar'. A friend, the late Marie-Anne Hobbs, whose native language was French, advised that *semenaire* is a time set aside for something, e.g. *semenaire de prière*, a time set aside for prayer. So here it appears to mean a time set aside for concentrated study before the examinations

[215] This was an example of the 'Nonconformist Conscience' at work. It is clear that there was great support for this councillor amongst chapelgoers in his crusade against the 'immorality' associated with the theatre. The minutes of the Quarterly Committee of the College, 27 November 1902, make reference to this case: 'That a letter of congratulation on the issue of the late trial at the Manchester Assizes be sent to Mr E. Holt, Chairman of the Watch Committee and Mr R. Peacock, Chief Constable, and we assure them of our sympathy in their great struggle with the forces of immorality in the city life.' Minutes in Hartley Collection, held at JRUL, Manchester.

[216] The Comedy Theatre (later known as the Gaiety Theatre) in Peter Street was built by Alfred Darbyshire for United Theatres Co. Ltd. in 1884, with a capacity of 2,500 and fitted with an orchestra pit. It was in use until 1947 and demolished in 1959. Music Hall and Theatre History website, www.arthurlloyd.co.uk [accessed 06.11.14].

[217] Sir Edward Marshall Hall KC (1858-1927) was a well-known barrister who had a formidable reputation as an orator. Born in Brighton, the youngest of

ten children of the doctor Alfred Hall, after Rugby School and St. John's College, Cambridge, he was called to the bar in 1883 and took silk in 1898. He successfully defended many people accused of notorious murders. In 1900 he was elected to Parliament as Conservative member for Southport, a seat which he retained until 1906. In 1901, in a libel case against the *Daily Mail,* he procured very large damages by suggesting an adjournment had been obtained for the purpose of finding out something detrimental about his client Hettie Chattell, an actress, a claim for which there was no foundation and for which he was severely criticised. Such irresponsibility and a tendency to quarrel with authority meant that he enjoyed greater popularity with the public than with members of his own profession. However, he was a powerful advocate with a commanding presence, and after several further murder cases, he became known as 'The Great Defender'. In late Victorian and Edwardian England, the public took a great interest in sensational court cases and barristers often became famous. C. Biron, revised by Mike Clarke, *ODNB.*

[218] In today's money that would be about £329,670.

[219] John Kinnish (1877-1949, see Diary n. 52 on 19 August).

[220] Rugby was a comparatively new game for the general public. It probably owed much to various ball games played since Elizabethan times, but the story, probably apocryphal, was that it originated in 1823 at Rugby public school, when William Ellis Webb 'with fine disregard for the rules of football as played at his time at Rugby School' first took the ball in his hands and ran with it. At first it was played at various public schools, then by Old Boys, clubs were formed and the expansion of the railways helped its spread to the general public. In 1863, after a series of meetings, rules for the game of football were drawn up and as a result, Blackheath, followed by other rugby clubs withdrew from the Football Association and the split occurred between rugby and soccer. The Rugby Football Union was formed in 1871 to standardize the rules and remove some of the more violent aspects of the game. In 1895 a dispute over professionalism and compensation caused Yorkshire and Lancashire to break away from the English Rugby Union to form the Northern Rugby Union, which became officially 'Rugby League' in 1922. Huw Richards, *A Game for Hooligans: A History of Rugby Union* (London: Mainstream Publishing, 2006).

[221] See Diary n. 80 and n. 81, concerning Rev. Albert Goodrich, Congregational Minister at Chorlton Road Congregational Chapel.

[222] Joseph Parker (1830-1902) was born in Hexham, Northumberland, son of Teasdale Parker, a stone-mason. The family were Congregationalists, apart

from a Wesleyan spell due to trouble in their chapel. After a basic education, as a young man he gained a reputation as a forceful Wesleyan preacher and advocate of temperance. In November 1851, he married the daughter of a local Wesleyan farmer, Ann Nesbitt, with whom he had twelve happy years before she died in 1863. Soon after his marriage, he wrote to John Campbell, minister of Whitefield Tabernacle, Moorfields, London, with a view to becoming a Congregational minister, and as a result became Campbell's assistant. After nine months he was called to the pastorate at Banbury, and then, five years later, in 1858, he became minister of Cavendish Chapel, Manchester, where he rapidly made himself a power in English Nonconformity. His publications included *Ecce Deus* and *The Paraclete*. He returned to London to be minister of the Poultry Church, and began the scheme for the erection of the great City Temple in Holborn Viaduct, which cost £80,000 and opened in May 1874. The 3000 seats at the City Temple were regularly filled for both Thursday and Sunday services. He was twice chairman of the Congregational Union of England and Wales (1884 and 1901). C. Binfield, in *BDE*, pp. 508-10.

[223] This story of a tsunami is still popular in addresses today.

[224] This large Congregational Chapel, built in 1848 and designed by Edward Walters, is no longer standing, but was pulled down to make way for university buildings. A 1905 photograph of Cavendish Street shows an impressive building with a spire, next to Pauldens, the department store. Schofield, *Manchester Then and Now*, pp. 98-9.

[225] Robert Charles Fillingham (1861-1908) was appointed vicar of St. Faith's, Hexham in Hertfordshire in 1891. In 1899, he caused controversy by protesting about what he called 'idolatry' at St. Paul's Cathedral, and in the same year protested on behalf of a Baptist minister, Theodore Beckett, who had been refused his legal right to carry out a funeral in the church graveyard by the vicar of Kettlebaston, Suffolk. In 1903 he wrote an open letter to Bishop Potter in New York in the *New York Tribune* (24 June 1903), after witnessing the ritualistic elements, such as vestments, incense and genuflection, during High Mass at the Church of St. Mary the Virgin in West Forty-sixth Street, which he declared to be in flagrant defiance of the discipline of the Church of England. *The New York Times* reporting on this, notes that for the past three years he has been working throughout England with a view to uniting all Protestants to protest against ritualism in the Protestant Church. In 1906 he was threatened with deprivation of his living by a church court unless he apologised and promised to reform, after he was said to have ordained a Nonconformist in an unconsecrated chapel. Websites: www.achurchnearyou.com/hexton-st-faith; and

archive.thetablet.co.uk/article/4th-november-1899/26/the-unity-of-the-anglican-church-two-different-voi; Newbury Frost Read, *The Story of St. Mary's*, anglicanhistory.org/usa/misc/read_story1931/1901.html; *New York Times*, 24.06.1903: query.nytimes.com [all accessed 14.11.14].

[226] Charles Leach (1847-1919) was born in Illingworth and grew up in Halifax. He began work in a mill at the age of eight, then served an apprenticeship as a shoemaker and set up in business. He became a Local Preacher in the New Connexion Methodist Church, and was given pastoral charge of a church in Sheffield, while attending Ranmoor Theological College, then sent to Ladywood Mission in Birmingham. There he began his Sunday afternoon lectures, which became so popular, attracting up to 4,000 people, that he had to use the Town Hall. He was ordained in 1877, and became a Congregational minister in 1881 when he took pastoral charge of Highbury Chapel in Birmingham. After a spell in London, he received the call to go to Cavendish Street Chapel in 1897. Here he was much involved with Passive Resistance, the movement protesting against the 1902 Education Act, as well as being active in the temperance movement. In 1908 stood for Parliament and was elected Liberal MP for Colne Valley. He retired from public life in 1915, and was the only MP ever to be removed from office on account of unsound mind (he was probably suffering from vascular dementia). J. B. Williams, *Worsted to Westminster: The Extraordinary Life of Rev. Dr Charles Leach MP* (Cambridgeshire: Darcy Press, 2009).

[227] See Diary n. 222 on Dr Parker.

[228] The City Temple was a Congregational Chapel on Holborn Viaduct, London, said to be the most important Nonconformist pulpit in Britain. The church was believed to have been founded by Thomas Goodwin around 1640, meeting first in Anchor Lane. Joseph Parker, then pastor at Cavendish Street Chapel in Manchester, was called to the pastorate in 1869. The congregation was at the time meeting in Poultry Chapel, but this was sold and the new building, called the City Temple, commissioned, and dedicated in 1873. Its size and furnishing, which included a splendid marble pulpit donated by the Corporation of the City of London, made it a leading Nonconformist chapel, to which the preaching of Joseph Parker drew congregations of thousands. Albert Clare, *The City Temple* (London: Independent Press, 1960); Hammond Dewey and Leslie Weatherhead, *The City Temple, Past, Present and Future* (London: The City Temple, 1958).

[229] Wood Street Mission is now a registered charity still helping to alleviate poverty in central Manchester, near Deansgate. It was established in 1869 by Methodist minister Alfred Alsop to alleviate the effects of poverty on

THE DIARY

children and families in the climate of widespread poverty and destitution. During the late nineteenth century and into the twentieth century, they ran a soup kitchen, a rescue society for neglected boys and a night shelter, distributed clothing, bedding and Christmas parcels, and organised trips to the seaside for children in the summer. Website: www.library.manchester.ac/searchresources/guidetospecialcollections/atoz/ woodstreet [accessed 12.11.14].

[230] In 1902, cities like Manchester rivalled London in importance, and world-class concerts were held there, which FCD was able to attend.

[231] Electric trams were introduced into Manchester from 1900. Previously they were horse-drawn; a report from 1893 showed that the 385 tramcars of the Manchester Carriage Company had required 3,583 horses (with all the resulting pollution of the streets). The municipal authorities took over the running of the trams from the private company in 1897. Schofield, *Manchester Then and Now*, p. 41; Hylton, *A History of Manchester*, p. 231.

[232] Dame Emma Albani was the stage-name of Marie Louise Emma Cecile Lajeunesse (1852-1930), a Canadian opera singer. She became first soprano at St. Joseph's Catholic Church, Albany, New York in 1866 and later adopted 'Albani' as her professional name in affectionate memory of America. *New Grove Dictionary of Modern Music and Musicians* (London and Toronto: J.M. Dent & Sons, 1924); Gladys Davidson, *Opera Biographies* (London: Werner Laurie, 1955), pp. 19-21.

[233] Ada Jemima Crossley (1871-1929), an Australian contralto, born at Tarraville, Victoria, to Edward Crossley, ironmonger, and Harriette, both from Northamptonshire, England. She had singing lessons with Madame Fanny Simonsen and made her first public appearance in Melbourne in 1889. She came to London in 1894 to study under Sir Charles Santley (see Diary n. 234) and then Madame Marchesi in Paris. Her London debut was in 1895 and she was soon in great demand for oratorios and festivals all over Great Britain; she gave five 'command performances' for Queen Victoria. Margery Missen, in *Australian Dictionary of Biography* vol. 8 (Manchester: Manchester University Press, 1981.

[234] Sir Charles Santley (1834-1922), an English baritone, was born in Liverpool and sang his first public solo at the Unitarian Chapel, Toxteth in 1848. At the age of fifteen, he was admitted to the second tenors of the Liverpool Philharmonic Society, and by the age of eighteen he was singing bass. During the years 1855-7, he trained in Milan under Gaetano Nava and in 1858 first sang in Mendelssohn's 'Elijah', of which he became a leading interpreter for over fifty years. For some years he devoted himself to Italian

opera, but later became better known at concerts and in oratorio. *Dictionary of Modern Music and Musicians* pp. 434-5; *Student and Singer: The Reminiscences of Charles Santley* (London: Edward Arnold, 1892).

[235] William Green (1868-1920) was a noted English tenor. A record produced to celebrate Sir George Grove and the Crystal Palace features artists who performed at the Crystal Palace, and includes William Green (tenor) singing from St. Paul, No. 40, 'Be thou faithful unto death,' by Mendelssohn in 1901. Website: www.symposiumrecords.co.uk/catalogue/1251 [accessed 30.11.15].

[236] Wilhelmina Neruda (1839-1911), was an international violinist and the second wife of Sir Charles Halle (1819-95), conductor and founder of the Halle Orchestra, who was twenty years younger than him and continued to perform in concerts after his death. She was born Vilenina Maria Franziska Nerudova, learned the violin at an early age and came to England as a child prodigy in 1849. In 1864 she married the Swedish composer and conductor Ludwig Norman, after which she performed under the name Wilma Neruda Norman. They separated in 1869, and in 1888 she married Charles Halle, whose first wife had died in 1866. After his death in 1895, the Prince of Wales raised a fund for his widow's benefit. She settled in Berlin, but returned to England every year for the Henry Wood concerts and the Halle concerts in Manchester. She had a graceful platform manner and it was said that her interpretation of Mendelssohn's E minor Violin Concerto was unsurpassable. Michael Kennedy, in *ODNB*.

[237] Adela Verne (1877-1952) was a notable English pianist and minor composer of German descent, born in Southampton to a musical family named Wurm, which she changed to Verne. She was considered one of the greatest woman pianists of her era. She toured with great success in many parts of the world. At age thirteen she made her debut in Tchaikovsky's Concerto No. 1 in B flat minor at the Crystal Palace. Tchaikovsky himself heard of this astonishing young prodigy and wanted to meet her. The following year she was introduced to Ignacy Jan Paderewski. He was so impressed with her playing that he predicted a great future for her. At his home in Switzerland she studied Chopin with Paderewski, as well as most of his own works, including the Sonata in E flat minor, the *Polish Fantasy* and the Concerto in A minor, the work with which she made her orchestral debut in New York. She appeared regularly at the Proms, and was the first British artist to give a solo recital at the Royal Albert Hall. https://en.wikipedia.org/wiki/Adela_Verne [accessed 08.11.14].

[238] See Diary n. 179.

[239] J. E. Roberts, co-pastor (see Diary n. 57 on 24 August).

[240] Maclaren was suffering ill-health in 1902-3, which meant that he had to retire in 1903. He preached his last sermon in 1904; however he lived until 1910 when he died at the age of 84.

[241] Hugh Price Hughes (1847-1902) was one of the leading Wesleyan ministers of the day. He was born in Carmarthen into a Methodist family; his grandfather, Rev. Hugh Hughes was a Welsh Methodist minister of distinction. He went to Richmond for training in 1866 and entered the ministry in 1867. He served for some years in the following circuits: Dover, Brighton, Stoke Newington, Mostyn Road (London), Oxford and Brixton Hill. As Superintendent in Oxford, he revitalised the circuit, then, during his years at Brixton Hill, he became editor of the *Methodist Times*. In 1888, he became the first Superintendent of the West London Mission, part of Methodism's response to *The Bitter Cry of Outcast London* (see Introduction n. 52) through its social and evangelistic work among the urban poor. He was a key figure in the Forward Movement of the 1880s and 1890s (see Diary n. 195 concerning Central Halls), and, as editor of the *Methodist Times,* he raised social issues around gambling, temperance and moral responsibility. His opposition to Parnell's adultery contributed to that man's downfall. He was committed to ecumenism and was one of the founders of the National Free Church Council, becoming the second President in 1896, and he became President of the Wesleyan Conference in 1889. His published sermons on social and ethical Christianity spoke of the combination of evangelism and social action that directed his life. Christopher Oldstone-Moore, *Hugh Price-Hughes: Founder of a New Methodism, Conscience of a New Nonconformity* (Cardiff: University of Wales Press, 1999).

[242] See Diary n. 222 on Dr Parker.

[243] Walter Graham (1841-1903) was a PM Minister who spent almost his whole ministry in the Manchester and Liverpool Districts. He was an example of the sort of person who, without the benefit of a college education, became a minister through the route of local preaching and oral examination. After Sunday School in Marple, and a conversion experience in his teens, in 1859, 'He was appointed to publicly preach the Word of God; this was done by the Quarterly Meeting without consulting our brother. There was nothing strange in this, for the members were expected to regard the call of the Church as the call of God.' He was recommended as 'a fit and proper person' for a travelling preacher in 1862, and then in 1863, after examination at the District Synod, appointed as a probationer minister to St Helens. He then served in the following circuits: Douglas,

Lymm, Preston, Castletown, Bradwell, Stockport, Blackburn I, Fleetwood, Liverpool I, Warrington, Lowton, Manchester V, Dalton, and Bury, before retiring to Manchester in 1903. *Aldersgate: The Primitive Methodist Magazine, 1899*; Leary, *Primitive Methodist Ministers*.

[244] Psalm 51:10.

[245] Moss Side Baptist Church on Stockton Street, is no longer standing, but the Youth Club, which was started in 1965 by members in the basement, thus called the 'Hideaway Club', continued in a building on the site for nearly fifty years. *Manchester Evening News* 23 January 2014. Website: www.manchestereveningnews.co.uk, [accessed on 14.11.14].

[246] Miss Agnes Paddon, presumably the same person, was a soloist at a Manchester Beethoven Society concert at the Gentlemen's Concert Hall, Manchester on 24 July 1897. The other soloists mentioned have been impossible to trace. Website [accessed on 19.11.14]: www.concertprogrammes.org.uk/html/search/verb/GetRecord/3998.

[247] Chorlton Road Congregational Chapel (see Diary n. 80 and n. 81).

[248] Perhaps this should be Nicholls? The reference may be to Agnes Nicholls (1876-1959), one of the greatest English sopranos of the twentieth century. She was born in Cheltenham and educated at Bedford High School, from where she won a scholarship to the Royal College of Music and was taught by Albert Visetti. In 1904 she married the conductor Hamilton Harty, who was to become famous as the director of the Halle Orchestra. She appears in concert programmes; for example on 9 November 1902 at a Sunday Afternoon Concert at Queen's Hall, Langham Place, a concert to mark the birthday of Edward VII, and at Worcester Music Festival in 1908. J. B. Steane, 'Agnes Nicholls', in *New Grove Dictionary of Music and Musicians*, vol. 17, p. 866; website: www.concertprogrammes.org.uk [accessed 9.1.2015].

[249] See Diary n. 233 on Ada Crossley.

[250] Ben Davies (1858-1943) was a Welsh tenor singer who appeared in opera with the Carl Rosa Opera Company as well as singing in oratorios. He was born at Pontardawe and as a boy sang in Caradoc's choir on a visit to Crystal Palace in 1873. In 1877 he won first prize at the Eisteddfod, and then from 1878 to 1880 studied at the Royal Academy of Music in London under Alberto Randegger and Signor Fiori. He made his debut in 1881 in *The Bohemian Girl*, and for ten years devoted his time to opera. Bernard Shaw, however, was said to be impressed by his performance in Mendelssohn's *Elijah* in 1892. He was a soloist in the London Handel Festival in 1894,

alongside Mme Albani, Charles Santley and others. Then in 1902 he was a soloist at the British and American Peace Concert at the Crystal Palace in London in commemoration of the South African War and in the same year performed in Mendelssohn's *Elijah* at the Sheffield Festival under Henry J. Wood. See A. Eaglefield-Hall, *Dictionary of Modern Music and Musicians*; *New Grove Dictionary of Music and Musicians*, vol. 7, p. 59.

[251] See Diary n. 234.

[252] Alexandra Park station.

[253] Soham station opened on 1 September 1879, serving the Ely, Fordham and Newmarket line; in 1898, this was absorbed by the Great Eastern Railway. His mother, Martha Ann, née Collen, came from Soham, Cambridgeshire, and her family still farmed there, so presumably the family were gathering there for Christmas.

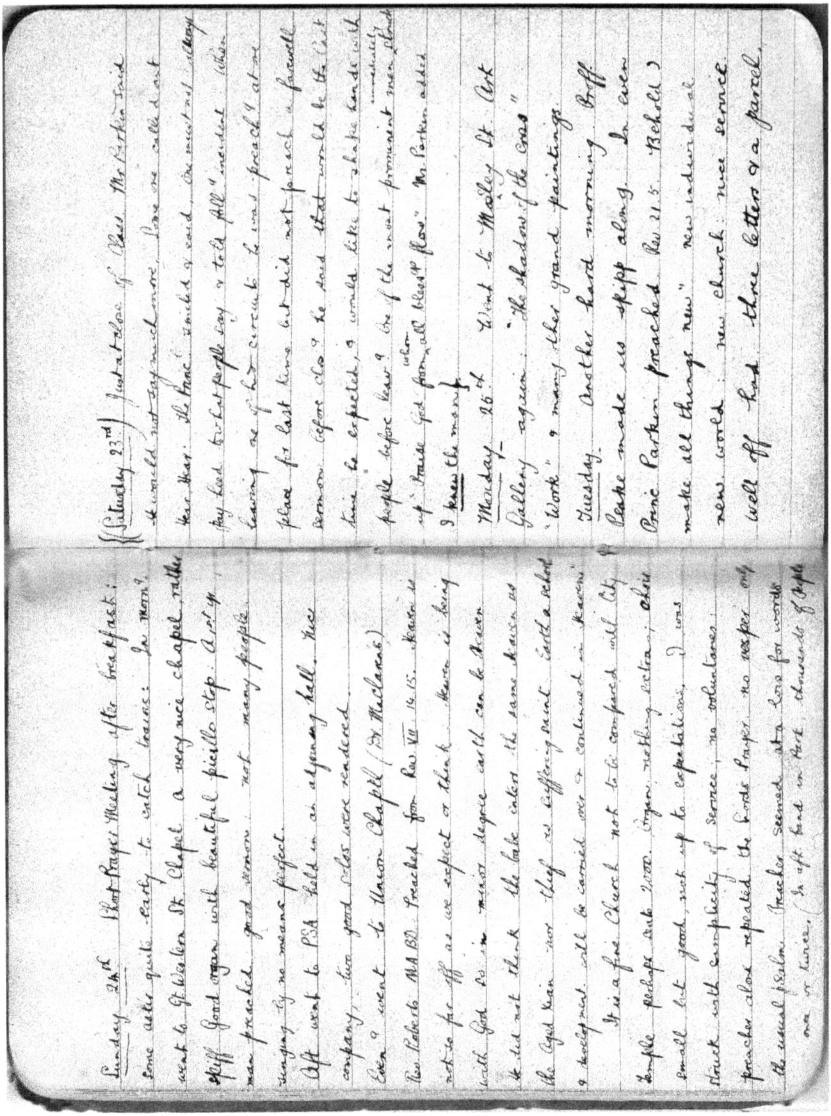

Sunday 24th Short Prayer Meeting after breakfast: some aster quite early to catch trains: In morn^g went to Gt Western St. Chapel a very nice chapel rather spiff Good organ with beautiful piccolo stop. A yg man preached good sermon: not many people singing by no means perfect.
Aft went to PSA held in an adjoining hall. Nice company, two good solos were rendered.
Even^g went to Union Chapel (Dr MacLaren's)
Rev. Roberts MA BD. Preached from Rev. VII. 14.15. Heaven is not so far off as we expect or think. Heaven is being with God so in minor degree earth can be Heaven He did not think the babe enters the same Heaven as the Aged Man nor thief as suffering saint. Earth a school & development will be carried over & continued in Heaven.
It is a fine Church not to be compared with City Temple perhaps seats 2000. Organ nothing extra; choir small but good, not up to expectations. I was struck with simplicity of service; no voluntaries: preacher alone repeated the Lords Prayer. no vesper only the usual psalm. Preacher seemed at a loss for words once or twice. (In aft band in Park thousands of people

(Saturday 23rd) Just at close of Class Mr Parkin said he would not say much more. Some one called out Hear Hear: the Princ^l smiled & said, One must not always pay heed to what people say & told foll^g incident When leaving one of his circuits he was preach^g at one place for last time but did not preach a farewell sermon. Before clos^g he said that would be the last time he expected, & would like to shake hands with people before leav^g. One of the most prominent men immediately struck up "Praise God from whom all bless^gs flow." Mr. Parkin added I knew the man.
Monday 25th Went to Mosley St. Art Gallery again: "The shadow of the Cross" "Work" & many other grand paintings.
Tuesday. Another hard morning. Proff. Peake made us skipp along. In even Princ Parkin preached Rev 21.5. "Behold I make all things new" new individual. new world: new church: nice service. well off had three letters & a parcel.

Excerpt from diary
(*Family collection*)

1

The Rev. James
Davidson
(*Family collection*)

His wife Martha Ann
Davidson (née Collen)
(*Family collection*)

The Collen Family of Soham, Cambridgeshire. Martha is third from right on the back row.
(*Family collection*)

Family Pictures

Cecil Davidson (brother)
(*Family collection*)

⑤

FCD (left) with his
brother Victor
(*Family collection*)

⑥

A typical postcard from Cecil to FCD
(*Family collection*)

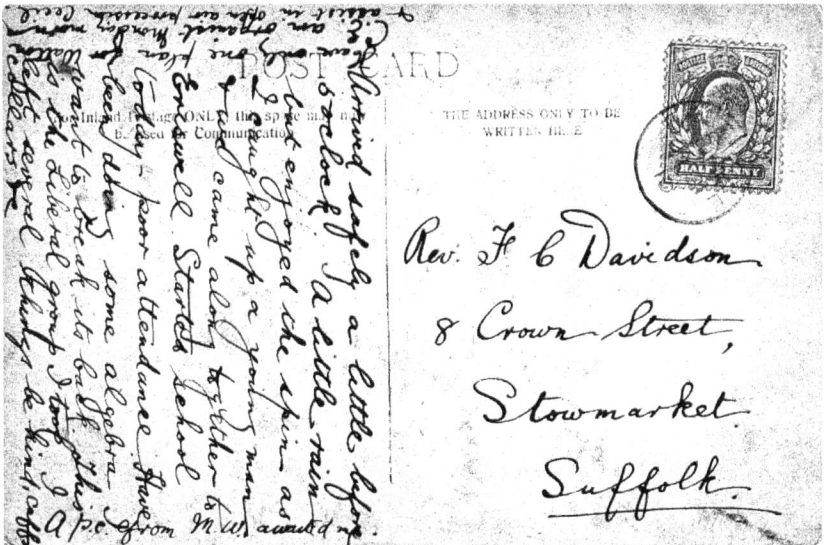

University of Cambridge

HONOUR   CERTIFICATE

THIS is to make known that

Frank C. Davidson

of

Fincham, Downham Market

is a STUDENT CERTIFICATED by the University of CAMBRIDGE, having passed the Examination for SENIOR Students prescribed by the Syndicate for conducting the Examination of Students who are not members of the University in December *1900*, and attained to the *Third* Class in Honours. Index-number, *345*.

Age, *17*, Centre of Examination, *Kings Lynn*.

The above-named Student satisfied the Examiners in ARITHMETIC, and in the *six* following subjects:

1. *Gospel;*
2. *English (Composition, Grammar, and Geography);*
3. *French;*
4. *Pure Mathematics;*
5. *Theoretical & Practical Chemistry, Electricity and Magnetism;*
6. *Freehand and Model Drawing*

W. Chawner VICE-CHANCELLOR.

FCD's Certificate (age 17)
(*Family collection*)

9

Soham Fen (ex-PM) Methodist Chapel (no longer in use),
photographed 20.10.2012 by Roger Larkinson

Soham Great Fen,
photographed 30.3.2014 by Roger Larkinson

Group of Primitive Methodists at Fakenham, including James Davidson, in the centre behind lady with impressive hat. (*Family collection*)

12

George and Mary Sculpher (parents-in-law)
and the farm in Hardingham (*Family collection*)

HALL. FARM   HARDINGHAM

Wedding couple, FCD and
Alice Mary Sculpher
(*Family collection*)

15

16

Hingham Chapel (ex-
PM), where the
wedding took place,
*photographed
15.4.2014 by
Roger Larkinson*

FCD, as a probationer minister, with an unknown person, perhaps a colleague, photographed in Biddulph, Staffordshire. (*Family collection*)

FCD as a student, with two fellow students, photographed in Manchester (*Family collection*)

FCD in garden
(*Family collection*)

(19)

(20)

FCD and Alice, with their first two children, Reg. and Morley
(*Family collection*)

Alice with Morley, Reg. and Kathleen (left to right)
(*Family collection*)

Alice and FCD with children Morley, Reg., Kathleen, and Dorothy (*Family collection*)

Manse, 19, Beaconsfield Road, Basingstoke, with Kathleen (*Family collection*)

Four generations
of Davidsons:
FCD (back left), Martha,
Reg., Dennis
(*Family collection*)

(24)

Gravestone, Soham
Cemetery, Cambridgeshire,
*photographed 13.1.2012 by
Rachel Larkinson*

TO THE MEMORY OF
MY BELOVED HUSBAND
REV. FRANK COLLEN DAVIDSON,
CALLED TO HIGHER SERVICE
NOV 5TH 1937 AGED 54 YEARS.
"UNDERNEATH ARE THE EVERLASTING ARMS"
ALSO OF ALICE MARY, HIS BELOVED WIFE
WHO DIED FEB. 9TH 1961,
AGED 76 YEARS.
"RESTING IN THY LOVE."

(25)

Stow Bedon Station, Norfolk,
the place where the journey to Manchester started.
(*by kind permission of Mr. John Moffoot of Stow Bedon*)

PRIMITIVE METHODIST COLLEGE, ALEXANDRA ROAD, MANCHESTER. (28)

The Manchester PM College in Alexandra Road
(*from the PM Minutes of Conference 1904, held at Englesea Brook*)

photographed 16.8.2012 by Roger Larkinson.

Two wings of the college, showing the rows of studies and bedrooms: *photographed 20.6.2015. by Rachel Larkinson.*

The lecture-hall, *photographed 20.6.2015. by Rachel Larkinson.*

College photo 1902: *(Family collection) FCD is third row back ninth from right.*

32

Some of the PM ministers mentioned in the diary

The Rev. William
Johnson

The Rev. Daniel
Neilson

The Rev. Robert Hind

The Rev. Arthur
Beavan

The Rev. John Harryman
Taylor

The Rev. Walter
Graham

*All these pictures appeared in the
"Aldersgate Magazine" (now held at
Englesea Brook) between 1899 and 1932.*

Dr. Arthur S. Peake

(*previously published in
"Workaday Preachers",
Methodist Publishing
House 1995, p.264*)

IN REVERENT AND LOVING MEMORY
OF
ARTHUR S. PEAKE M.A.,D.D.
BORN 1865 ☉ DIED 1929
TEACHER IN THIS COLLEGE 1892–1929
RYLANDS PROFESSOR OF BIBLICAL EXEGESIS
IN THE UNIVERSITY OF MANCHESTER
1904 – 1929
HE GAVE COUNSEL BY HIS UNDERSTANDING
WISE WERE HIS WORDS IN THEIR INSTRUCTION

Memorial inscription at the college (now a school),
photographed 20.6.2015 by Roger Larkinson.

Great Western
Street Methodist
Church (ex-PM)

(41)

*(Courtesy of Manchester Libraries, Information
and Archives, Manchester City Council)*

(42)

Oxford Road with MacLaren's chapel (Union Chapel)
(by courtesy of David Boardman)

THIS MEMORIAL.
ERECTED IN MEMORY
OF THE
Rev. ALEXANDER M‹LAREN, M.A., D.D.
IS PART OF THE PULPIT MADE
FAMOUS BY HIS GREAT MINISTRY IN
UNION CHAPEL, MANCHESTER, FROM 1869 TO 1903.
A MAN OF GOD, A PRINCE OF PREACHERS.

(43)

Maclaren's pulpit – in the chapel at Fallowfield.
See diary 11 August, 21 September and elsewhere:
photographed 16.8.2012 by Rachel and Roger Larkinson.

The Schoolroom, now a house, *photographed 18.2.2013 by Rachel Larkinson.*

Brookbottom: (see diary 10 August)

Window of the Chapel where FCD preached *photographed 18.2.2013 by Roger Larkinson.*

Brookbottom: countryside, *photographed 18.2.2013 by Roger Larkinson*

Manchester, The Royal Exchange 1886
(© *The Francis Frith Collection*)

Piccadilly, Manchester, 18 January 1906.
(*by courtesy of David Boardman*)

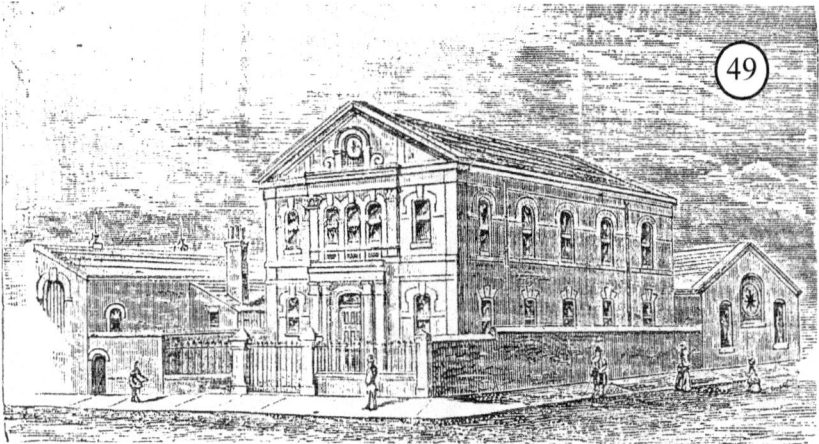

Oxford Street PM Chapel, Blackburn
(*Source: Mike Sumner, Blackburn with Darwen Library & Information Service*)

London Road PM Chapel, King's Lynn, mentioned in diary on 31 August. *(photograph supplied by Norma Virgoe)*

Manchester Town Hall
*photographed 14.2.2013 by
Rachel Larkinson.*

Manchester Cathedral, 1903 (*old postcard, in the public domain*)

53

Manchester, Whitworth Art Gallery,
photographed 16.8.2012 by Roger Larkinson.

Manchester Market Street from Cross Street, 17 December 1902
(*Courtesy of Manchester Libraries, Information and Archives,
Manchester City Council*)

54

1912 floods, Stowmarket, where FCD was minister 1908–12
and 1924–8. (*Family collection*)

Stowmarket PM Chapel. (*Family collection*)

Meeting at Stowmarket, with FCD (first left on back row) and his father James Davidson (sitting fourth from left, second row).
(*Family collection*)

A postcard of Station Road, Petersfield, where FCD was minister 1912–1915. The PM and Wesleyan Chapels, in close proximity, have been helpfully indicated!
(*Family collection*)

Fincham, Norfolk, one building the Chapel and the other the Schoolroom. FCD minister here 1915–1921. (*Family collection*)

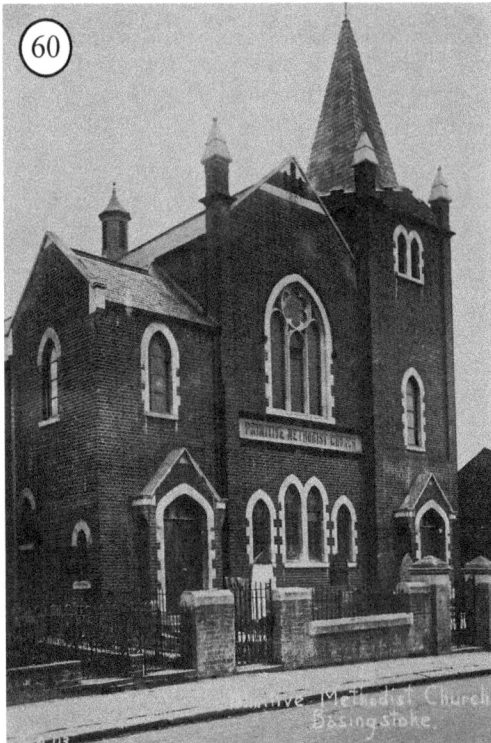

Basingstoke PM Chapel. FCD Minister 1921–4. (*Family collection*)

Swaffham PM Chapel. FCD Minister 1932–5.
(Photograph supplied by Norma Virgoe)

Buckenham Memorial PM Chapel, Fakenham,
where FCD was minister 1928–32.
(photograph supplied by Norma Virgoe)

Manea

Primitive Methodist
Chapel.
(*Family collection*)

FCD Superintendent
Minister from 1935 until
his death in 1937.

(63)

PRIMITIVE METHODIST CHURCH, MANEA.

High Street
(*Family collection*)

HIGH STREET, MANEA.

(64)

Annual Assembly, Bury St. Edmunds, 1909: James Davidson 2nd row back, fifth from left, FCD eighth from left. (*Family collection*)

65

PM Synod held at Aquila Road, Jersey, 1914.
FCD third row from back, first on right. Jersey
would be in the same district as Petersfield,
where he was stationed.(*Family collection*)

Middlesbrough Conference Group: FCD (seated on right),
Rev. F. A. Ingham,
Mr E. A. Harvey, J.P.,
Mr A. J. Deeks, Mr J. W. Able,
and Mrs J. B. Hart.
(*Family collection*)

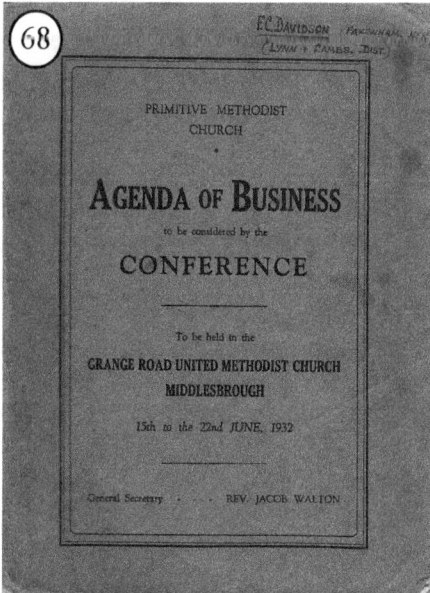

PRIMITIVE METHODIST
CHURCH

AGENDA OF BUSINESS
to be considered by the

CONFERENCE

To be held in the

GRANGE ROAD UNITED METHODIST CHURCH
MIDDLESBROUGH

15th to the 22nd JUNE, 1932

General Secretary - - - REV. JACOB WALTON

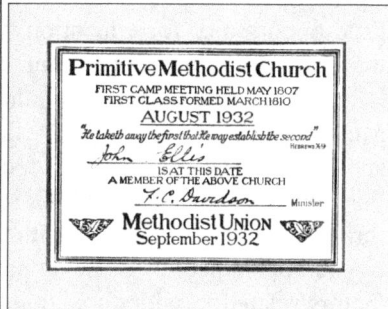

Primitive Methodist Church
FIRST CAMP MEETING HELD MAY 1807
FIRST CLASS FORMED MARCH 1810
AUGUST 1932
"He taketh away the first that He may establish the second"
Hebrews X:9
John Ellis
IS AT THIS DATE
A MEMBER OF THE ABOVE CHURCH
F. C. Davidson Minister
Methodist Union
September 1932

POSTSCRIPT

The diary ends at that point, but we know that FCD passed all his exams, completed his theological training and probation, went into circuit in 1904, and served in different circuits and districts, seeing unity come between the divisions of Methodism in 1932 and helping people through all the upheavals and amalgamations that involved. He attended both the last Conference of the Primitive Methodist church in Middlesbrough in June 1932 and the Uniting Conference held in London in September of that same year.

Most of his ministry was in East Anglia, where the Primitive Methodist movement remained strong. He was near his family there too, and maintained a correspondence with his brother, Cecil, who was a schoolteacher and also active in the church. One postcard speaks of books they had ordered and Cecil's role in playing the organ and providing music for a procession. When FCD was in Stowmarket, he hosted a Sunday School Convention at which his father, Rev. James Davidson, was one of the speakers. The picture we get is of the later years of the Primitive Methodist movement. Whereas his father, and many of his forbears on his mother's side, had responded to the fervent evangelical outreach of the earlier years and their lives had been turned around, FCD grew up in a family where Primitive Methodism, with its loyalties and responsibilities, was a way of life. In his younger days, the work was going forward, chapels were being opened in almost every village and hamlet in East Anglia, and, with the enthusiasm of camp meetings and rallies, there was much to nourish the faith and encourage commitment.

Indeed the Primitive Methodist Church played an important role in the history of Methodism in reminding the church of its roots in the open-air evangelism which drew in those outside the formal structures of church and empowered those from the working-classes, who had had little opportunity for education, to take leading roles in the service of the Lord. With its simple, democratic organisation, valuing clergy and laity alike, and its enthusiasm and fervour, it appealed to many existing Methodists and, by my grandfather's day, had members across the social spectrum, some of whom contributed considerable funds towards the building of chapels in most of the towns and villages where it thrived. However, as the twentieth century progressed, with the decline of membership due to the impact of the First World War and other factors related to wider social and cultural change,[1] it was realised that

150

there would be greater strength in unity. Already some of the strands of Methodism had united, and in 1932 the Primitives, Wesleyans and United Methodists joined together again to form the Methodist Church. All over the country congregations were urged to unite, though of course it meant that in some villages one or even two chapels had to close. In some places this went smoothly, but in others it would be many years before the buildings could be rationalised. Doubtless, this was a stressful time for the ministers who were working to help forward this change. FCD only saw the beginning of this process, but I feel sure he would have welcomed it, with his love of peace and the broadening of his outlook that took place at theological college.

The training of students was of course amalgamated. In Manchester, this meant that Hartley joined with Victoria Park College (which was United Free Methodist) to form Hartley Victoria College. Then in 1973 Conference decided that this college could no longer be maintained, but the work of training ministers in Manchester continued in an ecumenical partnership based on the Baptist premises at Martin Luther College. The further retrenchment in 2012-14 has brought to an end the great era of Methodist theological training in Manchester.

My grandfather's diary gives us a snapshot of life in 1902, both what was happening in Manchester and the life of a student in the theological college. We learn about the relationships between the Free Churches, as well as being acquainted with the leading preachers of the day and the themes of their sermons. Then, of course, as we read the diary, we get to know the personality of the writer, his love of art, music and sport, his meticulous recording of details, his modest, self-effacing nature, his enjoyment of jokes and the foolish side of student life, but above all, his hopes and fears for the work of the kingdom and the salvation of souls.

The stereotype of the Primitive Methodist has too long been fixed as plain and earnest, uneducated and unsmiling, so it is hoped that this authentic witness to the broader picture of life at their theological college will do something to redress the balance, and bring into sharper focus the contribution that the Primitive Methodists made to the on-going work of the whole Methodist Church.

APPENDIX 1:

STUDENTS 1902-3

First Year

John A. Ashworth	Frank Jones
James L. Baggott	John A. Kerswell
Richard J. Barrett	Herbert Lancaster
John H. Bedford	Laban Marston
John W. Bowden	Henry W. Matthews
Gerald E. Brown[2]	George W. Meadley
Henry Chamberlain	John Norton
Stanley K. Chesworth	James Palmer
James Clark	Harold W. Pope
David Cook	Seth Powell
Frank C. Davidson	Richard Rose
William Dawson	Thomas Shaw
John H. Dixon	Aaron Smith
William E. Farndale	Frederick T. Smith
Ernest E. Fisher	Edward A. Steen
William R. G. Fletcher	Frank Stoddard
Francis J. Harper	Arthur Wightman
Abraham Hill	Shirley Windram
William Hughes	William Woodley
Wallace P. A. Humphries	

Second Year

Charles T. Bishell	Ernest Metcalfe
T. Allison Brown	Charles Moore
Ernest S. Emmitt	John T. Morris
Philip A. Evans	Robert W. Nelson
Thomas A. Fairweather	Percy W. B. Oliver
G. Kirtley Fawell	James E. Phillipson
John R. Fell	Ernest H. Pitwood
Robert J. Fenwick	John W. Price
Lewis Hancock	John H. Robertshaw
Thomas B. Howard	William G. Rutherford
G. Stewart Hooson	Fred G. Saville
Frank U. Hull	John H. Thornley
John Kinnish	William F. Todd
Samuel A. Langham	Walter H. Wick
David Mayes	

APPENDIX 2:

THE CONSOLIDATED RULES
of the PRIMITIVE METHODIST CONNEXION
REVISED BY ORDER of the EIGHTY-THIRD ANNUAL
CONFERENCE held at HULL, JUNE 11-20, 1902[3]

'Just laws are no restraint upon the freedom of the good.'

Ministerial Education
THEOLOGICAL INSTITUTE AT MANCHESTER

Object

551. The object of this Institute is to assist young men in preparing for the ministry, by affording them such instruction as is essential to qualify them for their duties as Primitive Methodist Ministers.

Management

552. It shall be managed by a Committee, composed of the Principal, Tutors, Treasurer, Secretary, together with the Trustees and other Ministers and Laymen, who shall be appointed by the Conference in harmony with the Provisions of the Trust Deed.

553. The Committee shall meet monthly. The meetings held in February, May, August, and November shall be termed Quarterly Meetings. Each member of the Committee shall be informed of the business to be brought before the Quarterly Meeting.

554. The Principal, Tutors, Treasurer and Secretary shall be nominated by the Committee, but the appointment shall always be made by the Conference.

555. The Committees shall have power to remove any officer for incompetency or improper conduct, and to supply his place till the next Conference; but in all cases of dispute, appeals may be made to the General Committee.

556. The Committee shall appoint the Principal or some other representative, to attend the Conference, and supply such information as may be necessary respecting the students and the working of the Institute, and shall pay his expenses. It must forward to the Conference a report of its proceedings, with a balance-sheet of its accounts.

557. The Principal shall have under his supervision the health, morals, religious interests, preaching and other appointments of the students, and the general superintendence of the Institute.

558. The Principal's wife shall be the Matron, and shall have supervision of the household arrangements, management of servants, and custody of stores and furniture. Both Principal and Matron shall be responsible to the Committee for the proper discharge of their duties.

559. The Treasurer shall act under the direction of the Committee, and shall present his accounts with vouchers to the appointed auditors.

560. The Secretary shall enter all the Minutes of the Committee, and conduct the correspondence.

561. The Board of Management shall forward to each Conference a report of the Institute for the past year, and may send legislation to the Conference, (See Rule 61.)

Curriculum for Students

562. The Curriculum shall include the following subjects:–

a. First year's Students :– Systematic Theology, Pastoral Theology, including Homiletics, Logic, Church Government, Greek (New Testament), Old Testament Introduction, Old Testament Exegesis, Old Testament Theology, New Testament Introduction, New Testament Exegesis, New Testament Theology, History of Doctrine, Hebrew, and Classical Greek (optional).

b. Second year's Students: Systematic Theology, Pastoral Theology, including Homiletics, Psychology, Church Government, Greek, Old Testament Introduction, Old Testament Exegesis, Old Testament Theology, New Testament Introduction, New Testament Exegesis, New Testament Theology, History of Doctrine, Hebrew.

c. Third year's Students:– Hebrew, Classical Greek, Systematic Theology, Philosophy, Comparative Religion, Church History, Apologetics, Biblical Work.

d. German may be taken each year, but shall not be compulsory.

e. English language and English literature to be taught should the Principal and Tutors so decide.

563. Students who have graduated or matriculated at a University, or who may in the opinion of the Tutors be sufficiently advanced in any of the subjects specified, may be exempted from the study thereof, and have such others substituted as may be deemed most important.

564. The tutorial arrangements shall be as follow:–

a. The Principal shall teach Systematic Theology, Homiletics, and Church Government: The Tutors shall teach Old and New Testament Introduction, Old and New Testament Exegesis, Old and New Testament Theology, History of Doctrine, Hebrew, Greek, etc.

c. Additional tutorial assistance shall he provided by the Quarterly Committee as necessity may arise.

Students

565. No person shall be, admitted as a student unless he is a Local Preacher, and has been recommended by the Quarterly Meeting of the Station to which he belongs, by the Candidates' Examining Committee and the Conference.

566. On entering the Institute each student shall be required to sign a document stating (1) Whether he offers himself for Home, Colonial, or Foreign work. (2) That should he leave our ministry within six years of his entrance on probation he will pay to the Committee the sum of £30.

567. Students must remain in the Institute two years at least. The fees for each student shall be £15 per annum, which shall be paid half-yearly in advance.

568. Half-yearly examinations of the students shall be conducted in December and May by Examiners appointed by the Conference. Arrangements as to the method of conducting the examinations shall be made by the Tutors, Examiners, and Committee of Management.

569. In the examinations seven questions shall be prepared on each subject or book, five of which only shall be taken, and the Examiners shall indicate three which must be answered or attempted.

570. Candidates on the Reserve List, who so desire, shall be allowed to take part in the May Examinations with the students, and if they shall creditably pass the same they shall have equal claim to a Station with the students.

571. Each student who has finished his term and passed his examination satisfactorily may be appointed to a Station, and his probation shall commence at the Conference which gives him his appointment.

572. Students shall not be appointed to Stations before the end of their term without the concurrence of both the General Committee and the Committee of the Institute.

Maintenance

573. In addition to students' fees, the Institute shall be supported by grants from Connexional funds, donations and legacies. (See Rules **367, 370.**)

APPENDIX 3:
EXAMINATION PAPERS
AT THE MANCHESTER COLLEGE

[A selection of the questions on the examination papers of 1897, which are held at the John Rylands Library in Manchester, is reproduced here to give some idea of the breadth and depth of the studies undertaken at the college in the late nineteenth and early twentieth century.]

Manchester Primitive Methodist College
Examination Papers, May 1897

General Rubric: Each student is expected to answer five questions only in each department, the three questions indicated by footnote to form part of the five. Students must number right-hand side, write only on one side, date and sign the paper, tack the sheets together with the printed questions attached to the first sheet, and then return. Should any Examinee overlook another student's papers or have recourse to any book for answers, or speak to another student, his examination shall at once cease. The full value of each satisfactory answer is four marks. Two hours will be allowed for each paper except Systematic Theology for which two hours and a half may be taken.

SYSTEMATIC THEOLOGY, BANKS[4]
FIRST AND SECOND YEAR

1. Define the term 'Church.' How often does Christ use it, and with what significance? How does He represent what we mean by the term 'Church?'
2. 'Of all the transformations which history has witnessed, none is more complete or startling than that of the New Testament presbyter.' Comment on this.
3. How and by whom was Sacerdotalism imparted into the Christian Church? What terms do Christ and his Apostles use to denote the Christian Ministry?
4. 'Sacraments are holy *signs* and *seals* of the covenant of grace.' Comment on this.
5. 'In transubstantiation, it is not a miracle we are asked to believe, but a contradiction.' Comment.
6. Say what is meant by Millenarianism, and what scriptural authority there is for such a belief.

7. Give some account of the theory known as 'Probation after death.'
Questions 1, 3, and 5 to be attempted.

LOGIC
FIRST YEAR

1. Distinguish between the Categorical and Hypothetical Judgment and say what kind of assertion the latter enables you to make.
Examine the following:– If the plague continues men will die; men die; therefore the plague continues.
2. Give an instance of the complex constructive dilemma. Discuss the value of the dilemmatic argument as a means of ascertaining truth.
3. What is a fallacy? Give an instance of *Petitio Principi* and say to what class it belongs.
4. Distinguish between Deductive and Inductive reasoning. What is meant by Imperfect Induction? Can it give certain knowledge?
5. Indicate the use and limits in reasoning of the principle known as the 'Uniformity of Nature.'
6. Give an account of Mill's doctrine of Causation.
7. Define the following terms:– Synthesis, hypothesis, theory, method.
Questions 1, 2, and 4 to be attempted.

GERMAN
FIRST YEAR

1. What meanings may the following pronouns have? – Euch, ihrer, euer, ihr.
2. Conjugate *wollen* in the past tense, conditional mood, and *mögen* in present tense, conditional mood, giving the English in every case.
3. Derive the following verbs:–Rannte, dachte, wusste, blies. Conjugate *geben* in the imperative.
4. Conjugate *sich freuen* in the imperfect indicative, and *regnen* in the past conditional. Give the English.
5. Compare the following adverbs:– Hoch, wenig. Give the construction of nach, laut, durch.
6. Put into German the following portion of the Lord's prayer:– Our Father ... daily bread. (*Heiligen,* to hallow.)
7. Put into German:–
  (a) I am cold, thou art warm, we are pleased, they are sorry.
  (b) I have resolved not to quarrel again with the teachers.
Questions 1, 6, and 7 to be attempted.

GERMAN

SECOND YEAR

1. Translate:–

Ich hatte Holz gefällt im Wald, da kommt Mein Weib
gelaufen in der Angst des Todes. Der Burgvogt lieg' in
meinem Haus, er hab' Ihr anbefohlen, ihm ein Bad zu rüsten
Drauf hab' er Ungebührliches von ihr Verlangt, sie sei
entspringen mich zu suchen. Da lief ich frisch hinzu, so wie
ich war, Und mit der Axt hab' ich ihm's Bad gesegnet.

2. Prefix the article, singular and plural, to the following:– Engel, Lust,
Eis, Feld, Tier, Zeit, Kahn, Tag, See (a lake), Herz, Freund.

3. Translate:–

Mich jammert nur der Vater – er bedarf
So sehr der Pflege, und sein Sohn ist fern.
Der Vogt ist ihm gehässig, weil er stets
Für Rech und Freiheit redlich bat gestritten.
Drum werden sie den alten Mann bedrängen,
Und Niemand ist, der ihm vor Unglimpf schütze,
– Werde mit mir, was will, ich musz hinüber.

4. Parse the verbs in question 1, giving the principal parts of each verb.

5. Translate:–

Laszt ihn mitt Gott hinüber gehn, Dort drüben
Ist kein Verräther – So verabschent ist
Die Tyrannei, dasz sie kein Werkzeug findet.
Ach der Alzeller soll uns nid dem Wald
Genassen werden und das Land erregen.

6. Parse fully the verbs in 5.

7. Put the following portion of the Lord's prayer into German:– Our
Father ... that trespass against us. (*Heiligen,* to hallow; *Vergeben,* to
forgive; *Schuld,* a transgression.)

Questions 1, 2, and 7 to be attempted.

OLD TESTAMENT EXEGESIS

FIRST AND SECOND YEAR STUDENTS

1. Write notes on the following, with reference to the context:–

(a) 'Behold, I will stir up the Medes against them, which shall not
regard silver, and as for gold, they shall not delight in it.'

(b) 'But thou art cast forth away from thy sepulchre like an abominable branch, clothed with the slain, that are thrust through with the sword, that go down to the stones of the pit.'

(c 'For the fields of Heshbon languish, and the vine of Sibmah; the lords of the nations have broken down the choice plants thereof.'

2. Write notes on the following, with reference to the context:–

(a) 'Neither shall he have respect to that which his fingers have made, either the Asherim, or the Sun-images.'

(b) 'I will be still, and I will behold my dwelling place; like clear heat in the sunshine, like a cloud of dew in the heat of harvest.'

(c) 'And her pillars shall be broke in pieces, and they that work for hire shall be grieved in soul.

3. Write notes on the following, with reference to the context:–

(a) 'Prepare ye slaughter for his children for the iniquity of their fathers; that they rise not up, and possess the earth, and fill the face of the world with cities.'

(b) 'Her nobles flee unto Zoar, to Eglathshelishiyah.'

(c) 'O thou my threshing, and the corn of my floor; that which I have heard from the Lord of hosts, the God of Israel, have I declared unto you.'

4. Discuss the date of the prophecy about Moab, (Is. 15-16.)

5. To what date has the burden of the wilderness of the sea (Is. 21:1-10) been assigned? Discuss the different views.

6. What do you know of the following:–'Ophir,' 'Jazer,' 'The Cities of Aroer,' 'Noph,' 'Sargon.'

7. Write brief notes on the following: 'Faces of flame,' 'The Golden City,' 'Day Star and Son of the Morning,' 'Battle Shout,' 'As the years of an hireling,' 'He cried as a lion.'

Questions 3, 4, and 5 must be attempted.

OLD TESTAMENT THEOLOGY

FIRST AND SECOND YEAR STUDENTS

1. Mention some of the proofs to show that the Semites passed through the Totem Stage.

2. What was the nature of the vegetable offering?

3. Give an account of the levitical law of the trespass or guilt offering.

4. What explanations have been given of the imposition of hands? Which seems to be correct?

5. Describe the use made of the blood in the sacrifices.

6. What views have been taken of the phrase "the goat for Azazel?" Which seems the most probable?
7. In what senses is the term "Messianic prophecy" used.
Questions 1, 5, and 7 to be attempted.

NEW TESTAMENT THEOLOGY
FIRST AND SECOND YEAR STUDENTS

1. Show that the doctrines of the pre-existence and divinity of Christ were taught by Paul.
2. Examine the view that Paul was quite indifferent to the facts of the earthly life of Christ.
3. How would you deal with the charge that Paul's doctrine of justification by faith is immoral, because it makes God pronounce a man innocent when his character does not correspond to this declaration?
4. Show that Paul's absolute statements as to the ideal character of the Christian life are held alongside of a full recognition of the actual facts of experience. Is he guilty of any real inconsistency?
5. Examine the teaching of Paul as to the position of the Holy Spirit within the Godhead.
6. Write brief notes on 'the earnest of the Spirit,' 'the Spirit of His Son,' 'whereby we cry Abba Father.'
7. Reproduce the teaching of Paul on the Church as the body of Christ.
Questions 1, 5, and 7 to be attempted.

NEW TESTAMENT EXEGESIS
FIRST AND SECOND YEAR

1. Write notes on the following passages with reference to their context:–
   (a) 'And if Christ is in you, the body is dead because of sin: but the spirit is life because of righteousness.' (8:10).[5]
   (b) 'For the creation was subjected to vanity not of its own will, but by reason of him who subjected it.' (8:20).
2. Write notes on the following passages, with reference to their context:
   (a) 'And be not fashioned according to this world; but be ye transformed by the renewing of your mind.' (12:2)
   (b) 'Whatsoever is not of faith is sin.' (14:23)

3. Write brief notes on the following:– 'Condemned sin in the flesh,' 'the mind of the flesh,' 'anathema,' 'reasonable service,' 'coals of fire.'
4. Give an outline of Paul's argument in Chapters 9-11.
5. How does Paul deal with the question of the relation of Christians to the State? Show the wisdom of his advice at the time when he was writing.
6. What theories have been propounded in explanation of the two-fold benediction in Chapter 16? Criticise them.
7. What were the views held by the ascetic party in the Church of Rome and in what way were they met by St. Paul?
Questions 1, 4, and 6 to be attempted.

OLD TESTAMENT INTRODUCTION
FIRST AND SECOND YEAR

1. Explain the scheme of history adopted by the compiler of the book of Judges. By what leading ideas was he governed?
2. On what grounds has the account of the institution of the monarchy in 1 Samuel be *(sic)* analysed into two narratives?
3. Give an account of the two narratives of the introduction of David. Discuss the bearing of the Septuagint on this.
4. Compare the Septuagint account of the development of Saul's jealousy of David with that in our present Hebrew text.
5. Mention some of the ideas and phrases characteristic of the compiler of the books of Kings.
6. 'Behold! Is it not written in the Book of the Song.' What is the true title of the book referred to? In what circumstances does the mention of it occur? Quote, if you can, the passage that has been recovered.
7. Give an account of the double narrative of the division of the Kingdom found in the Septuagint.
Questions 2, 5, and 6 to be attempted.

NEW TESTAMENT INTRODUCTION
FIRST AND SECOND YEAR

1. Discuss the objection to the authenticity of the Gospel of John, based on the expression 'high-priest in that year.'
2. What positive arguments may be adduced to prove that the writer of the Gospel was a Jew?
3. From what source did John probably derive his doctrine of the Logos?

4. How would you meet the objection to the authenticity of the Fourth Gospel based on the difference in tone and style between the speeches of Christ in it and those in the Synoptists?

5. Give a brief outline of the external testimony to the authorship of the Acts.

6. What argument in favour of the historical character of the Acts has been drawn from the author's use of political terms? Give examples.

7. What argument was based by the Tübingen School on the parallelism in the Acts between Peter and Paul? Criticise it.

Questions 2, 4, and 6 to be attempted.

PSYCHOLOGY
SECOND YEAR   TIME: TWO HOURS

1. How are forms of thought regarded:
   (1) By the Logician?
   (2) By the Psychologist?

2. The term Judgment has a wider meaning in Psychology than in ordinary usage. Comment.

3. Explain carefully:
   (1) Self-consciousness.
   (2) Perception of ideas.

4. In what respect do sensations differ from each other? What is meant by remoteness from sensation?

5. Indicate the relation of Psychology to the expression of emotion.

6. Distinguish between voluntary reflex and random action.

7. State and illustrate what is meant by an act of volition.

Questions 1, 2, and 6 to be attempted.

APPENDIX 4:
SYLLABUS for PROBATIONER MINISTERS[6]

[The following extracts from the Connexional syllabus for probationers gives a good picture of the breadth and depth of the studies required in the first years of ministry. There were less demanding alternatives for those who had not had the benefit of the college education and had studied at home, which was clearly envisaged as possible; students who did not attend college did not have to study in Hebrew or Greek, but there was offered an alternative in English.]

First year
1. Holy Scripture: in Hebrew – Judges 13-16 inclusive [a handwritten note adds: 'or Driver's[7] Joel and Amos', presumably in English].
2. Holy Scripture: in Greek – Luke 1-10 inclusive, with Fairbairn's *Studies in the Life of Christ*.[8]
3. Comparative Religion: Menzies' *History of Religion*.[9]
4. Psychology: James' *Textbook of Psychology*[10] pages 1-238

Second year
1. Holy Scripture: in Hebrew – Deuteronomy 1- inclusive.
2. Holy Scripture: in Greek – Acts of the Apostles 1-12, with Page's notes.[11]
3. Theology: Orr's *The Christian View of God and the World*, (Lectures I-IV).[12]
4. Psychology: James' *Textbook of Psychology*, pages 239-end.[13]

Third year
1. In Hebrew: Amos.
2. In Greek: Epistle to the Ephesians.
3. Theology: Orr's *The Christian View of God and the World*.[14]
4. Philosophy: Watson's *An Outline of Philosophy* to p. 302.[15]

Fourth Year
1. In Hebrew: Psalms 42-51 inclusive.
2. In Greek: Epistle to the Hebrews.
3. Bruce's *Apologetics*: Introduction and Books I and II.[16]
4. Political Economy: Walker's *Brief Textbook of Political Economy*.[17]
[The minimum mark required to pass was 60%.]

APPENDIX 5:
EXTRACTS FROM MINUTES OF
PROBATIONERS' COMMITTEES 1905-9

[These extracts show how Probationers' examinations were a considerable hurdle for young ministers straight out of college, with all the demands of circuit life upon them. The report of 1908 indicates that questions were being asked about the effectiveness of the Probationary Studies in developing the abilities of ministers.]

163

[1905] Minute 18: That we recommend the Conference to appoint Rev. A. L. Humphries MA to fill the vacancy caused by the death of Rev. D Nielson (*sic*) BD.

Resolution from Probationers' Committee
to Conference this year (1908):
'That this committee, being convinced that in the course of ministerial probation, as well as in the preliminary stages of candidature and college-training, greater regard in the interests of our church be paid not simply to ability to pass literary examinations but to the possession of high Christian character, evangelistic zeal, marked preaching capacity, and pastoral efficiency, earnestly recommends the Conference to appoint a special committee to consider the whole question, and to prepare, if necessary, legislation supplementing the present examination schemes by such arrangements as shall secure that greater importance is at every stage, prior to a man's entrance into the full ministry, attached to his possession of those elements of practical ministerial usefulness Rev. referred to.'

... Rev. A. T. Guttery seconded the resolution. '... He did not wish to see their pulpits filled with pedants or with philosophers ... On the other hand he did not wish to see the pulpits degraded by morbid sensationalism ... There were some prices too great to pay for full chapels. He wanted all the culture the Hartley College could give them. He was proud of the College and thanked God for the wealth that had provided it. No man was prouder of Dr Peake than he was. (Cheers.) What made the doctor so welcome in their pulpit was not so much his great learning as his simple spiritual faith in God.' (Much cheering.)

(Rev. J. Harryman Taylor spoke as secretary of the committee.)

Rev. W. Johnson, Principal of the Manchester College, was given permission to address the Conference. In reply to a statement that there were sometimes one hundred students in the College with nothing to do on a Sunday, he pointed out that they had never had more than 89 students in the College and every Sunday from 25 to 28 were engaged in preaching. Besides, they also carried on mission work in connection with two of the Manchester Circuits ... In concluding he evoked ringing cheers by declaring that in our church we did not want a professional man but a prophet.

Dr Peake, whose rising was the occasion of a remarkable demonstration, supported the resolution ... He told how at a re-union of his old students at Newcastle, he had told them he would far rather, if he were to be remembered at all, be remembered as a spiritually-minded man than as an intellectual force ... This was the spirit that was lying behind their work at the College. They were trying to turn out men who would have every qualification for success in the Christian ministry ... He had always pointed out to them that whilst there was much to be acquired as a basis for a successful ministry, they should not bring the processes of the lecture room into the pulpit, for there they had to deal with the great moral and spiritual realities ... In concluding Dr Peake appealed to his hearers to discourage a spirit of depreciation of their work at the College. It did not help them and they must remember that they were all seeking to achieve the same thing, which was the spiritual salvation and moral uplifting of the world.

APPENDIX 6:
DETAILS OF LOCAL PREACHERS' TRAINING

[It is interesting to compare what was asked of ministerial students in college and at home with the training and expectations of Local Preachers. These were people who would usually work the hours of a full-time job before they could begin the studies required by the church. Although they are not expected to reach the same academic standards as ministerial students, yet it is impressive to see the amount of detailed organisation, including the assignation of tutors that went Into their training, and the level of theological understanding required.]

Central Committee held Sept. 21 1904
Present were[18]:– R. Bryant, J. Walford, H. Yooll, F. Pickett, W. Lee, M. P. Davison, M. T. Wigham, W. Foak, J. L. Gerard, H. Jeffs, G. Carter.

Resolved that ... the following tutors be appointed, with the respective subjects, to the Correspondence Classes[19]:–

Rev. J. Tongue BA, Frodingham Rd, Scunthorpe, via Doncaster.
Subject – *Key to Unlock the Bible*, by Dr Beck   1s 6d[20]

Rev. G. Parkin, BD, 37,Werneth Hall Rd, Oldham.
Subject – Theology – *Christian Doctrine*, by Dr Townsend or Gregory[21]

Rev. W. Lee BA
Subject – *Old Testament & its Contents* (Guild)
by Prof. Robertson DD   6d[22]

Rev. A. L. Humphries, MA, King's Rd, Alexandra Park, Manchester.
Subject – *New Testament & its Writers* (Guild)
by Dr McClymont,[23] 6d

Rev. Matt. Johnson, Hutton le Hole.
Subject – *Landmarks of Church History* (Guild)
by Prof. Cowan DD,[24] 6d

Rev. R. W. Keighley, 39, Melton Road, Leicester.
Subject – H. B. Kendall's *Prim. Methodist History and Polity*[25] 6d

Rev. F. Jeffs, 174, Ellesmere Road, Sheffield.
Subject – Homiletics: *Preaching*, by Rev. G. Fletcher[26]
(Wesleyan Book Room) 1s 6d

Mr J. J. Webb, 38, East Road, West Ham.
Subject – Gill's *Grammar*[27] 1s[28]

[The following material has been added in pencil]
Rev. G. C. Normandale – Key to Bible
A. L. Humphries – Teaching of Jesus
M. P. Davison – New Test. and Writers
R. P. McPhail – Christian Writers
H. Jeffs – Bible Manners and Customs

Special Committee held at Aldersgate St., 11 Feb. 1909
Present: Brothers Carter, Bourne, J. Welford, F. Pickett, W. Lee BA,
M. J. Wigham, A. L. Humphries MA, H. Yooll.
Res[olve]d that ...

5. That the proposed legislation be sent to the General Committee
& Conference of 1909.

What shall be done to further promote the training and equipment
of Local Preachers?

(1) – That rule 162 Consolidated Minutes, p. 29, be altered to read:–
'But no person must be admitted on the plan as Exhorter till he has
been examined by the Circuit as to his religious experience, devotional
habits, and knowledge of the Scriptures, and has also filled up the
printed form issued by the Book Committee ...'

(2) That rule 163 Consolidated Minutes p. 29, be altered to read:–
'In addition to giving satisfactory answers to the queries in sections a-h,
the candidate before being placed on full plan shall undergo regular
examinations by the Circuit in Theology, Homiletics, Biblical
Introduction, PM Polity, Christian Evidence, and English Grammar, the

text books on those subjects being those appointed for the primary course of the Local Preachers' Correspondence Classes (which appear monthly in the 'Teacher and Preacher') and approved by Conference.'

(3) That the following section be inserted under rule 163:–

'(A) Circuits are strongly urged to earnestly recommend all candidates for the plan to sit for the Yearly General Examinations prepared by the Central Training Council, and held in District Centres in the last week in April. Those who have been received as accredited Local Preachers should also be urged to complete the primary course, and go forward to the advanced course of study.'

Reasons: 1.Uniformity of method, 2. Greater efficiency in Equipment.

Signed:– H. Yooll, Secretary.

Primitive Methodist Church:
Darlington & Stockton District Local Preachers'
Training Committee Correspondence Classes, 1909-10.

The arrangements for the coming Session are now complete.

You are asked to select one, two, or three of the following Text Books, and order them as early as possible. Your Minister can supply them.

Questions on each book will appear in the "Teacher and Preacher" each month, September to March. Send your answers *to me* during the last week of the month if possible.

Your answers will be corrected by one of the sub-tutors and returned to you.

Let me know which books you will study, and I will send you full rules and suggestions. Reply early.

Please make the Classes known as much as you can. Send me the names and addresses of any likely Students.

TEXT BOOKS

1. *Primitive Methodist History and Polity*, by Kendall   4½d[29]
2. *Preaching (Homiletics)*, by Fletcher[30]   1s 1½d
3. Gill's *English Grammar*[31]   1s
4. *Our Lord's Teaching*[32] Guild Series   6d
5. *Christian Evidences*[33]   6d
6. *New Testament and its Writers*[34]   6d
7. *Manners and Customs of the Bible*[35]   6d
8. *Christian Character*   6d
9. *Christian Doctrine*   6d

Advanced Section
10. *Unto This Last*, by Ruskin[36]
11. *Romans*, by Garvie[37]   2s 6d
12. *Outlines of Theology*, by Clarke[38]   5s 8d

APPENDIX 7:
EXTRACT FROM THE LECTURES OF A. S. PEAKE

[At the John Rylands Library, there is a bound copy of the lectures of Prof. A.S. Peake, handwritten at first, then, as time went on, printed and duplicated. The following brief extract gives some idea of the breadth of the material and the approach to learning that he used.]

Old Testament Introduction [handwritten]
Reading List:
Driver: *Introduction to the Literature of the Old Testament*[39]
Robertson Smith: *Old Testament in the Jewish Church*[40] *Wright: Introduction to the Old Testament*[41]
Kuenen: *Hexateuch*[42]
Wellhausen: *Prolegomena*[43]
Articles in *Encyclopaedia Britannica* and Smith's *Dictionary of the Bible*[44]
The Old Testament Introduction embraces the study of the text of Scripture, its accuracy and integrity, of the authorship and authenticity of the several books and of the documents that have been taken up into those of composite authorship. It deals further with the collection of these books into the OT canon. It cannot be too strongly stressed that the problems of the OT and the NT are almost wholly different. It is often asserted that advanced criticism of the OT will run the same course and meet the same fate as the Tubingen criticism of the NT The truth or falsity of this prediction can only be proved by time. But it is well to remember that the cases are so dissimilar that a valid argument can only be proved by time ...
[He goes on to say that there is very little evidence beyond internal evidence for the OT but a wealth of external evidence for the NT.]
Headings: The Text of the Old Testament, The Authorship of the Books, The Hexateuch, The Books of Samuel, The Books of Kings, The Poetical Books.

Old Testament Theology August 1892 [handwritten]
Introduction, The Prophets, Outline of the History of the Religion of Israel, The Nature of God, The Future Life, Sacrifice, Hebrew Sacrifices, Messianic Prophecy.

New Testament Theology

Pauline Theology
Books:–
Bruce: *St Paul's Conception of Christianity*[45]
Stevens: *The Pauline Theology*[46]
Pfleiderer: *The Pauline Theology*[47]
Sabatier: *The Apostle Paul*[48]
Everett: *The Gospel of Paul*[49]
Weizsacker: *The Apostolic Age*[50]
Somerville: *St Paul's Conception of Christ*[51]

Sources, Doctrine of God, Doctrine of Human Nature, Doctrine of Sin, Preparation for Christ, Person of Christ, Work of Christ, Individual Appropriation of Salvation, Holy Spirit, The Church.
Epistle to the Hebrews.

APPENDIX 8:

WORK WITH CHILDREN

[In the Diary, reference is made to Sunday Schools and the work that was being done with the large number of children who attended (e.g. 31 August: 'In afternoon I went over to Princes Street School (Day and Sunday) ...'). In the Methodist Archives at JRUL is a copy of the Second Reading Book for Primitive Methodist Sunday Schools. The Preface gives an idea of the aims and purposes of the work.]

PREFACE
The design of this Second Reading Book is to supply easy reading for a class next in order below the Scripture Classes. The lessons are all taken from the Holy Scriptures and may be divided into three Sections: The Creation of the World and the Fall of Man – some Miscellaneous Readings – and, lastly an abridgement of the Life and Death of our Lord Jesus Christ. These lessons are chosen with a view to the securing of two objects:– First, supplying easy reading for the practice of children as a preparation for the general reading of the Scriptures; and,

Secondly, for the purpose of imparting some of the most important instructions of those Scriptures to the youthful mind. If it be said, Why should the lessons be published in a separate form seeing they are taken exclusively from the Bible? we only reply:– That it is a convenience to have lessons ready chosen to our hands; and further, that some degree of uniformity is secured thereby in the teaching of our Schools generally, which we hold to be a matter of considerable advantage.

[1] See Robert Currie, Alan Gilbert and Lee Horsley, *Churches and Church-goers; Patterns of church growth in the British Isles since 1700* (Oxford: Oxford University Press, 1977), pp. 30-32 and 115-7 on the effect of war.

[2] Gerald E. Brown does not appear in Leary, *Directory of Primitive Methodist Ministers* or *Who's Who in Methodism 1934*, so it seems this should read Oswald E. Brown, who does appear in those publications and is not on this list.

[3] Published: London: Robert Bryant, 48-50 Aldersgate Street, 1902. This document was kindly supplied by Dr Clive Field.

[4] This is a reference to the book by John Shaw Banks (1835-1917), *A Manual of Christian Doctrine* (London: T. Woolmer, 1887). See Diary n. 200 above on Banks.

[5] All the Bible references in this paper are from Romans.

[6] Where possible, in this and subsequent appendices, textbooks have been identified from the British Library catalogue.

[7] Samuel Rolles Driver (1846-1914) was Regius Professor of Hebrew at Oxford. His commentaries on Joel and Amos were produced in 1897.

[8] A. M. Fairbairn, *Studies in the Life of Christ* (London: Hodder and Stoughton, 1881).

[9] Allan Menzies, *History of Religion* (Published by Murray, 4th ed., 1911).

[10] William James, *Textbook of Psychology* (1892).

[11] T. E. Page and A. S. Walpole, *The Acts of the Apostles with Introduction and Notes* (London: Macmillan, 1895).

[12] James Orr, *The Christian View of God and the World*, being the Kerr lectures for 1890-1 (Edinburgh: Elliott, 1893).

[13] See Appendices n. 8.

[14] See Appendices n. 10.

[15] John Watson, *An Outline of Philosophy*, first published in 1895 under the title *Comte, Mill and Spencer: An Outline of Philosophy* (Glasgow: J. Maclehose/New York: Macmillan, 1898).

[16] Alexander Balmain Bruce, *Apologetics; or Christianity Defensively Stated* (Edinburgh: T & T Clark, 1892).

[17] Francis Amasa Walker, *Political Economy* (London: MacMillan & Co., 1883).

[18] The name 'A. Wingate/' (written thus) is at the top left of first page – uncertain significance. The names of those recorded as present are written top right.

[19] Presumably 'Classes': original somewhat unclear.

20   One shilling and sixpence.

21   "Gregory" added later in pencil.

22   Sixpence.

23   James Alexander McClymont, *The New Testament and its Writers* (London: A. & C. Black, 1893).

24   Henry Cowan, *Landmarks of Church History to the Reformation* (London: A. & C. Black, 1894).

25   Holliday Bickerstaffe Kendall, *History of the Primitive Methodist Church* 2 vols (London, Joseph Johnson, Primitive Methodist Publishing House; revised ed. 1919).

26   George Fletcher (tutor in the Wesleyan College, Richmond), *Chapters on Preaching: a Manual for the Guidance of Young Preachers* (London: Charles Kelly, 1902).

27   Gill's School Series, *Elements of Analysis of English Grammar* (London: Simpkin, Marshall & Co., 1876).

28   One shilling.

29   See Appendices n. 25.

30   See Appendices n. 26.

31   See Appendices n. 27.

32   James Robertson DD, *Our Lord's Teaching* (Edinburgh: R. & R. Clark, Guild and Bible Class Textbooks, 1897).

33   Alexander Stewart, *Handbook of Christian Evidences* (Edinburgh and London: A. & C. Black, Guild and Bible Class Textbooks, 1895).

34   See Appendices n. 28.

35   G. M. Mackie, *Bible Manners and Customs* (Edinburgh: R. & R. Clark, Guild Textbooks, 1900).

36   John Ruskin, *Unto This Last, four essays on the first principles of political economy* (New York: J. Wiley & Son, 1862).

37   Albert Ernest Garvie, *Romans*, in the series 'The Epistles Anthology' (New York: H. Frowde, 1906).

38   William Newton Clarke, *An Outline of Christian Theology* (New York: Charles Scribner's Sons, 1898).

39   S. R. Driver, *Introduction to the Literature of the Old Testament* (Edinburgh: T. & T. Clark, 1892).

40   W. Robertson Smith, *The Old Testament in the Jewish Church – 12 Lectures on Biblical Criticism* (New York, D. Appleton and Company, 1881).

[41] Charles Henry Hamilton Wright, *An Introduction to the Old Testament* (London: Hodder & Stoughton, 1898).

[42] Abraham Kuenen, *An Historic-Critical Enquiry into the Origin and Composition of the Hexateuch (Pentateuch and Joshua)* translated from the Dutch by P. H. Wicksteed (London, Oxford: Macmillan, 1886).

[43] Julius Wellhausen, *Prolegomena to the History of Israel* (Edinburgh: A. & C. Black, 1885).

[44] William Smith, *Dictionary of the Bible* (London: John Murray, 1863).

[45] Alexander Balmain Bruce, *St Paul's Conception of Christianity* (Edinburgh: T & T Clark, 1894).

[46] George Barker Stevens, *The Pauline Theology – A Study of the Origins and Correlation of the Doctrinal Teachings of the Apostle Paul* (New York: Scribner, 1898, 1892).

[47] Otto Pfleiderer, *Lectures on the Influence of the Apostle Paul on the Development of Christianity, delivered in London and Oxford in April and May 1885* translated by J. Frederick Smith, 1885. This is in the Rare Books Room at Cambridge University Library and is the closest to the given title to be found.

[48] Louis Auguste Sabatier, *The Apostle Paul* translated by A.M. Hellier (London: Hodder & Stoughton, 1891).

[49] Charles Carroll Everett, *The Gospel of Paul* (London: J. Clarke and Co., 1893).

[50] Carl von Weizsacker, *The Apostolic Age of the Christian Church* 2 vols (London: Williams and Norgate, 1894 & 1895).

[51] David Somerville, *St Paul's Conception of Christ: Or, the Doctrine of the Second Adam. The Sixteenth of the Cunningham Lectures* (Edinburgh: T & T Clark, 1897).

BIBLIOGRAPHY

Primary Sources

Agenda of Business, PM Conference, Middlesbrough, 1932.

Cambridgeshire Archives, Shire Hall, Cambridge:
Quarterly Meeting Minute Book (Manea Circuit) 1926-38; Castle Street, Cambridge PM Chapel, Baptism Register (1824-61); Soham Fen Chapel Centenary Publication (1972).

Cambridgeshire Times (12 November 1937).

Congregational Yearbook (1905, 1920, 1922).

Letters, papers and photographs of Alice Mary Davidson (Family collection, Cambridge).

Ministers and Probationers of the Methodist Church 1957 (London: Methodist Publishing House, 1957).

Primitive Methodist Theological Institution/Hartley Victoria College Archives, held at JRUL, Manchester.

Minutes of the Methodist Conference (1933, 1937, 1938, 1943, 1944, 1947, 1949, 1950, 1953, 1955, 1958-61, 1966-68, 1971, 1973, 1985).

Minutes of the Primitive Methodist Conference (1902, 1906, 1915, 1918, 1919, 1932).

Minutes of the (Wesleyan) Methodist Conference (1903, 1917, 1921, 1930, 1932).

Sunderland PM Institute Archives, JRUL, Manchester.

The Howard Journal of Criminal Justice, 22 (Oxford: Wiley-Blackwell, 1983).

The Primitive Methodist Magazine/Aldersgate Magazine (1899, 1906, 1909, 1913, 1919, 1922, 1932).

United Methodist Church Minutes of Conference (1915).

Uniting Conference Agenda (London 1932).

Who's Who in Methodism 1933 (London: Methodist Times and Leader, 1933).

Secondary Literature

Abram, William Alexander, *Parish of Blackburn, County of Lancaster: A History of Blackburn, Town and Parish* (Blackburn: J. G. & J. Toulmin, 1877).

An Encyclopedia of New Zealand, edited by A. H. McLintock (Wellington: Owen, Govt. Printer, 1966).

Anderson, Paul, *Railways of Lincolnshire* (Oldham: Irwell Press, 1992).

Archer, John H. G., *Art and Architecture in Victorian Manchester* (Manchester: Manchester University Press, 1985).

Australian Dictionary of Biography Vol. 8 (Manchester: Manchester University Press, 1981).

Banks, John, *Samuel Francis Collier* (Peterborough: Foundery Press, 1996).

Beattie, Derek, *Blackburn: A History* (Lancaster: Carnegie Publishing, 2007).

Bebbington D. W., *The Nonconformist Conscience* (London: George Allen and Unwin, 1982).

Bradshaw's Descriptive Railway Handbook of Great Britain and Ireland (Oxford: Old House, 2012).

Brash, W. Bardsley, *The Story of our Colleges* (London: Epworth Press, 1935).

Briggs, Asa, *Friends of the People: The Centenary History of Lewis's* (London: B. T. Batsford, 1956).

Brodbribb, John, *The Main Lines of East Anglia* (Oxford: Ian Allan Publishing, 2009).

Burnett, John, *A History of the Cost of Living* (Harmondsworth: Penguin Books, 1954).

Clare, Albert, *The City Temple* (London: Independent Press, 1960).

Clifton-Taylor, Alec, *The Cathedrals of England* (Norwich: Thames and Hudson, 1967, reprinted 1979).

Currie, Robert, Gilbert, Alan and Horsley, Lee, *Churches and Church-goers: Patterns of Growth in the British Isles since 1700* (Oxford: Oxford University Press, 1977).

Davidson, Gladys, *Opera Biographies* (London: Werner Laurie, 1955).

Dewey, Hammond, and Weatherhead, Leslie, *The City Temple in the City of London: Past, Present and Future* (London: The City Temple, 1958).

Dictionary of Music and Musicians (London and Toronto: J. M. Dent & Sons Ltd, 1924).

Dingle, A. E., *The Campaign for Prohibition in Victorian England* (London: Croom Helm, 1980).

Egremont, Max, *Balfour: A Life of Arthur James Balfour* (London: Weidenfeld and Nicolson, 1998).

Farnie, Douglas A. and Jeremy, David J. (eds), *The Fibre that Changed the World* (Oxford: Oxford University Press, 2004).

Foreman-Peck, James (ed.), *New Perspectives on the Late Victorian Economy* (Cambridge: Cambridge University Press, 1991).

Gordon, W. J., *Our Home Railways,* 2 vols (London and New York: Ian Allan Ltd., 1910).

Hartwell, Clare, *Manchester,* Pevsner Architectural Guides series (New Haven: Yale University Press, 2002).

Hylton, Stuart, *A History of Manchester* (Andover: Phillimore 2010).

Larson, Timothy (ed.), *Biographical Dictionary of Evangelicals* (Leicester: Inter-varsity Press, 2003).

Leary, W., *Directory of Primitive Methodist Ministers and their Circuits* (Loughborough: Teamprint, 1990).

Lysons, Kenneth, *A Little Primitive* (Buxton: Church in the Marketplace Publications, 2001).

Machin, G. I. T., *Politics and the Churches in Great Britain 1869-1921* (Oxford: Clarendon Press 1987).

Magnusson, Magnus (ed.), *Chambers Biographical Dictionary* (Edinburgh: Chambers 1990).

McCurdy, Leslie, *Attribute and Atonement: The Holy Love of God in the Theology of P. T. Forsyth* (Carlisle: Paternoster, 1998).

McIntyre, Ian, *Robert Burns: A Life* (London: Constable, 2009).

Milburn, Geoffrey, *A School for Prophets* (Manchester: Hartley Victoria College, 1981).

Milburn, Geoffrey, *Primitive Methodism* (Peterborough: Epworth Press, 2002).

Milburn, Geoffrey and Batty, Margaret, *Workaday Preachers: The Story of Methodist Local Preaching* (Peterborough: Methodist Publishing House, 1995).

Mitchell B. R., *British Historical Statistics* (Cambridge: Cambridge University Press, 1988).

Munson, James, *The Nonconformists: In Search of a Lost Culture* (London: SPCK, 1991).

Neill, Stephen, *A History of Christian Missions* (Harmondsworth: Penguin Books, 1964).

Norgate, Tomas L., *From Pedagogy to Photography: The Life and Work of John Willian Righton* (Petersfield: 613 Books, 2008).

Oldstone-Moore, Christopher, *Hugh Price-Hughes: Founder of a New Methodism, Conscience of a New Nonconformity* (Cardiff: University of Wales Press, 1999).

Oxford Dictionary of National Biography (Oxford: Oxford University Press, 2004).

Oxford Dictionary of Quotations (London/Oxford: Book Club Associates /OUP, 1981).

Oxford English Dictionary (Oxford: Oxford University Press, 1971).

Peake, Leslie S., *Arthur Samuel Peake: A Memoir* (London: Hodder and Stoughton, 1930).

Pevsner, Nikolaus and Harris, John, *Lincolnshire* (Harmondsworth: Penguin Books, 1964, repr. 1973).

Pritchard, John, *Methodists and their Missionary Societies 1760-1900* (Farnham, England: Ashgate, 2013).

Railway Clearing House Atlas of England and Wales (Surrey: Ian Allan Publishing, 2001).

Richards, Huw, *A Game for Hooligans: A History of Rugby Union* (London: Mainstream Publishing, 2006).

Robbins, Keith, *England, Ireland, Scotland, Wales: The Christian Church 1900-2000* (Oxford: Oxford University Press, 2008).

Ritson, Joseph, *The Romance of Primitive Methodism* (London: Edward Dalton, 1909).

Robert, Dana, *Occupy Till I Come: A. T. Pierson and the Evangelization of the World* (Grand Rapids, MI: Eerdmans, 2003).

Royle, Edward, *Modern Britain: A Social History 1750-2011* 3rd ed. (London and New York: Bloomsbury Academic, 2012).

Santley, Charles, *Student and Singer* (London: Edward Arnold, 1892).

Schofield, Jonathan, *Manchester Then and Now* (London: Batsford, 2009).

Selby, William Boothby, *Life of Andrew Martin Fairbairn* (London: Hodder & Stoughton, 1914).

Sell Alan P., *Confessing and Commending the Faith* (Cardiff: Cardiff University Press, 2002).

Steward, Cecil, *The Stones of Manchester* (London: Edward Arnold Ltd, 1956).

Tatton-Brown, Tim and Crook, John, *The English Cathedral* (London: New Holland Publishers, 2002).

The New Grove Dictionary of Music and Musicians edited by Stanley Sadie (London: Macmillan 2001).

Unwin, Mrs George and John Telford, *Mark Guy Pearse* (London: Epworth Press, 1930).

Vickers, John A. (ed.), *A Dictionary of Methodism in Britain and Ireland* (Peterborough: Epworth Press, 2000).

Virgoe, Norma and Williamson, Tom, *Religious Dissent in East Anglia* (Norwich: Centre of East Anglian Studies, 1993).

Wilkinson, John T., *Arthur Samuel Peake: A Biography* (London: Epworth Press, 1971).

Williams, J. B., *Worsted to Westminster: the extraordinary life of Rev. Dr Charles Leach MP* (Cambridgeshire: Darcy Press, 2009).

Wilson, John F., ed., *King Cotton: A Tribute to Douglas A. Farnie* (Lancaster: Crucible Books, 2009).

Wragg, David, *A Historical Dictionary of the Railways of the British Isles* (Barnsley: Wharncliffe Books, 2009).

Frank Davidson grew up in rural East Anglia, moving to different manses as the work of his father, a Primitive Methodist minister, required. Just before his nineteenth birthday he set off on the journey to Manchester, a vibrant, prosperous and cultured city, dubbed 'Cottonopolis' for the wealth coming in through the cotton trade, but also a place of great poverty, deprivation and industrial pollution. Here he was to train for the ministry himself at the Primitive Methodist Training Institute. During his first four months he kept a diary, reproduced here, which gives an insight into the impact of this experience and the life and times of people in 1902.

College, Chapel and Culture in Edwardian Manchester

Editor Rachel Larkinson

ISBN 978-0-9928762-1-0

90000

9 780992 876210

COLLEGE, CHAP
AND CULTURE
EDWARDI
MANCHEST

The diary of Frank C. Davidson in his first of training for the Primitive Methodist Min

edited by Rachel Lark

www.ingramcontent.com/pod-product-compliance
Lightning Source LLC
La Vergne TN
LVHW051631080426
835511LV00016B/2282